School Tax Elections

School Tax Elections

Planning for Success
in the New Normal

Third Edition

Don E. Lifto and Barbara Nicol

ROWMAN & LITTLEFIELD
Lanham • Boulder • New York • London

Published by Rowman & Littlefield
An imprint of The Rowman & Littlefield Publishing Group, Inc.
4501 Forbes Boulevard, Suite 200, Lanham, Maryland 20706
www.rowman.com

6 Tinworth Street, London SE11 5AL, United Kingdom

British Library Cataloguing in Publication Information Available

Library of Congress Cataloging-in-Publication Data Available

978-1-4758-4595-2 (cloth : alk. paper)
978-1-4758-4596-9 (pbk. : alk. paper)
978-1-4758-4597-6 (electronic)

∞™ The paper used in this publication meets the minimum requirements
of American National Standard for Information Sciences—Permanence
of Paper for Printed Library Materials, ANSI/NISO Z39.48-1992.

Dedication

In Memoriam of
J. Bradford Senden
1949–2016

I first met Brad Senden in San Francisco in 2000. We both attended the National Conference on Education hosted by the American Association of School Administrators (AASA). I presented on the topic, "So You Lost the Election . . . Now What?" and Brad conducted a workshop on using random-sample surveys to test the feasibility of school tax elections. As fate would have it, I attended Brad's presentation, and he found his way to mine. A quick chat in the hall was followed by an extended conversation over a delicious San Francisco lunch, and the foundation was laid for what became a sixteen-year friendship and professional relationship.

Back to Brad's presentation at AASA—I was more than a little impressed that Brad's random-sample quota survey methodology had achieved wins at the California polls at a significantly higher percentage than the national average. Of particular interest was the fact that at that time, California required a two-thirds supermajority to win an election. Although I was very familiar with the use of phone surveys to help plan and execute school tax elections, Brad's work at the Center for Community Opinion and Political Designs was far more sophisticated than what I had experienced.

Since our chance meeting in San Francisco, Brad and I coauthored two books and published twelve articles on planning and executing school tax elections. We also collaborated on many state and national presentations on this shared area of interest. Barbara Nicol, my coauthor for this book, also partnered with Brad and me on numerous referendum projects in which she developed and implemented informational campaigns in support of future school tax elections.

In July 2016, I joined Brad's family and friends in grieving his much-too-early passing. Brad's obituary read in part, "He was an author, speaker, photographer, athlete, classical music lover, and gourmet chef, as well as a devoted father and grandfather." Although his PhD was in English, Brad's academic pursuit did not get in the way of what was no doubt a genetic predisposition to immerse himself in politics—whether that be state and national initiatives or running (unsuccessfully) for mayor of Indianapolis, Indiana. For most of his career, Brad's interest focused on local politics and, more specifically, helping school districts win tax elections when voter approval was needed to gain operating money for teaching and learning or permission to issue bonds for school construction projects.

In memoriam of J. Bradford Senden, we dedicate this book in hopes that the combined wisdom and experience of those gone and those still here can fuel the passion that drives us—strengthening our public schools and the children, families, and communities they serve.

Don E. Lifto
January 2019

Contents

Foreword   ix
Daniel A. Domenech

Introduction   xi

1   Research to Practice   1

2   Voter File and Target Structure   11

3   Looking Back to Plan Forward   21

4   Geovisual Demographic Mapping   33

5   Community Survey: Testing Feasibility   43

6   Ballot Structure   67

7   Ongoing and Strategic District Communication   75

8   Planning Framework   97

9   Campaign Leadership and Organization   111

10   Executing the Campaign   119

A Final Thought   149

Appendix A   151

Appendix B   153

Bibliography   157

About the Authors   165

Foreword

Executing a successful school tax referendum can be one of the most important—yet also one of the most difficult—responsibilities a school system leader faces. School leaders must not only be adept at planning for school needs; they also must be political salespersons who can convince the public—from a foundation of clear, concise, and compelling information—that the needs of students and our public schools periodically require that citizens put aside their private interests to support the public good.

Given that most states don't allow taxpayer dollars to be used for advocacy efforts, this requires finesse, collaboration, and strategy. Whether a school tax referendum involves a vote to seek more operating money, to fund technology initiatives, or to issue bonds for school construction, effective leadership is essential to winning on election day.

In *School Tax Elections: Planning for Success in the New Normal, Third Edition*, Don Lifto and Barb Nicol provide a recipe for success. They offer practical, research-based advice for preparing for an election campaign, anticipating potential challenges, and managing the process to increase the chances for a successful outcome.

They divide their comprehensive planning model into the key elements of school tax referenda. These elements include using a research-based approach, targeting messages strategically using voter files and demographic maps, analyzing and learning lessons from past elections, seeking community feedback through surveys, crafting effective ballot questions, using effective communications to target and engage the public, writing a detailed communications plan, and coordinating the work of the school district with that of an effective advocacy group working to identify and gain the needed "yes" votes to win the election.

In addition to these core lessons, the revised and updated third edition of *School Tax Elections: Planning for Success in the New Normal* provides expanded and updated information about strategies and best practices when it comes to community engagement and communication planning.

Today, school tax referenda are often won and lost by small margins. With such little room for error, anyone involved in leading, planning, and executing such an initiative should read this book carefully.

Daniel A. Domenech
Executive Director
American Association of School Administrators
Arlington, Virginia

Introduction

"Education officials need to furnish leadership in school elections . . . an unsuccessful election reduces educational opportunities for students" (Kimbrough & Nunnery, 1971, p. 4). Who can argue with this simple statement? The challenge is that providing effective leadership is not that easy. Research and practice have yet to yield an election formula that always produces winners.

Whether it is a request for technology upgrades, building construction and renovation, or more operating money, each election type and context is unique. There's no guarantee that a set of campaign strategies that are wildly successful in one district will not fail in your community. If successful campaigns were *not* such a delicate balance of science and art, the key to success would have long since been discovered, resulting in significantly more success on election day.

In planning this book, the title includes a reference to the *new normal*. Changing demographics, the pervasive influence of social media, and an increasingly contentious political climate are key variables affecting school tax referenda today versus when the first edition was published in 2004.

The growing demographic of alumni parents provides us with a wonderful example of the evolving nature of school tax elections and the complex components involved in their success. In this context, alumni parents are residents who had one or more children in a school district in the past but the last child has graduated. Many are baby boomers and are either retired or approaching retirement. Our research identifying the "tight-fisted" character of alumni parents does not bode well for school tax elections.

In most phone surveys conducted to evaluate the feasibility of a school tax referendum, alumni parents are generally *less supportive* than residents who have never had children in a school district. In digging deeper into this counterintuitive finding, data suggest a combination of attitudes drive this reality: alumni parents' collective belief that they have "done their fair share" when their children were in schools as well as the fact that many suffer from economic anxiety in their preretirement phase of life. The size and disposition of this group of voters are significant challenges for school leaders.

A recent case in Rochester, Minnesota, illustrated another *new normal* reality and challenge, which is focused on technology-savvy opposition groups. Included within a broad suite of print and electronic informational media produced by the school district to explain its referendum proposal was an 8.5 × 11, two-sided informational flier. As one would expect, the color scheme, font, logo, and layout were consistent with all of the district's media, including its website. An antitax opposition group essentially did a "save as" of Rochester's flier and produced a "vote no" piece that was a visual mirror image of the district's literature with different messages. In looking at the two side by side, it would appear that both came from the school district. Although Rochester was successful in getting a restraining order restricting further distribution of the copycat flier, the damage it caused was done.

Broad use of social media, of course, amplifies the challenge for school leaders to respond effectively to opposition messages. In training school administrators to plan and execute school tax referendums, we often refer to an Allstate Insurance television commercial. In the *new normal*, one crabby old guy with a Facebook or Twitter account can produce significant *mayhem* in your school tax referendum (the "guy" reference here is intentional, as opposition most frequently emanates from men).

In terms of the political and tax climate, school leaders are affected by two *new normal* realities. Broadly affecting the political climate in local referendums are the increasingly polarized nature of the electorate, decreased civility, and tightening tax tolerance. Like the dark clouds of a thunderstorm, school tax referendums are often affected by these broader climate issues.

Specifically related to tax tolerance, some prereferendum feasibility surveys contain the following statement: *I would never vote for a tax increase, no matter the amount or how the money raised would be used.* Respondents are asked if they strongly agree, agree, disagree, or strongly disagree with that statement. In most school districts, somewhere between 15 and 25 percent of residents agree they would not support any increase in taxes for any purpose. In recent years, we have seen two subtle but important changes: the average percentage of voters agreeing with the no-tax sentiment has increased somewhat and the percentage of residents strongly agreeing has also crept up.

This "perfect storm" of demographic, economic, political, and technological drivers will make it considerably more difficult to meet the operational and facility needs of public school students going forward, as many states report lower passage rates for school tax issues in recent years compared to what had been the norm over time. This challenging reality makes it even more important that school leaders understand and have the ability to effectively use research and best practices when seeking approval on election day.

Our book is intended to form a marriage between research and successful practice, presenting a comprehensive planning model for school leaders who are preparing for and conducting school tax elections. Information presented emphasizes systems and strategies rather than specific campaign tactics. Avoiding a myopic focus on tactics allows school leaders to elevate their thinking to a more comprehensive and long-range vision of election planning. Each of the chapters elaborates on one or more of the 10 elements in our comprehensive planning model (see figure I.1). Use of this model has

Figure I.1   Comprehensive Planning Model

reaped success in all types of school districts, from New Jersey to California, and we hope that it brings you success on election day as well.

ELEMENT 1
Research to Practice

Although there is no pat formula for success, school leaders should not be discouraged from rolling up their sleeves, digging in, and becoming students of sound research and successful practices. In the final analysis, there is no better road map to a successful election. In fact, university libraries are replete with dissertations documenting that winning campaigns use research-based strategies to a *greater extent* and *more effectively* than unsuccessful elections.

Understanding the research on school tax elections and thoughtfully implementing these strategies are the foundations of winning campaigns. The Internet provides the means for school leaders to review relevant research with simple word searches through the Open Access site at https://oatd.org/.

ELEMENT 2
Voter File and Target Structure

The voter file and target structure represents the district's master election dossier, which details essential information about a campaign's key resources—the voters. By integrating files of registered voters, parents, preschool families, past supporters, and other key groups with commercial demographic and predictive databases, the district's campaign is provided with a powerful tool for planning, canvassing, targeting messages, and implementing get-out-the-vote strategies.

ELEMENT 3
Postelection Analysis

It is important to keep one eye on the rearview mirror as you drive toward your next election. A thorough understanding and analysis of your district's prior elections is a prerequisite to effectively executing your next campaign. By integrating data from voting records with the parent file, school leaders can gain a more precise understanding of past voter participation, the extent to which it got its main targets to cast a ballot, and how the demographics of turnout need to change to ensure success in a future referendum.

ELEMENT 4

Geovisual Demographic Mapping

Geovisual demographic mapping provides a visual depiction of key voter information and targets. Parent data can be merged with registered voter files and other demographic and predictive databases to map the district's vital voter target structure to the rooftop. Geovisual demographic mapping provides the district and campaign committee with a powerful resource to support communications, door-to-door canvassing, and getting out the vote.

ELEMENT 5

Scientific Survey

Aligning the community's values and appetite for spending with what the school district actually needs and puts on the ballot is paramount to success. A well-designed, scientific, random-sample survey of registered voters can help the school district evaluate the feasibility of a future tax election both in terms of the content of a potential ballot proposal and the current climate for a tax increase.

ELEMENT 6

Ballot Question

When the voters enter the voting booth, what will they see? In most states, ballots can contain a single proposal or multiple questions. Will each of the ballot questions be freestanding (i.e., winning or losing on its own merits), or will passage of the second or third question be contingent on the first proposal getting a thumbs-up? The decision about the content and structure of the ballot is critical and must be guided by the district's election history and the results of a scientific survey.

ELEMENT 7

Ongoing and Targeted Communications

Developing a compelling message and directing it to parents just prior to an election used to be good enough, but not anymore. In today's election environment, providing high-quality, ongoing communication throughout the year is essential. The election campaign builds on this foundation by developing core and subordinate messages and targeting them to various audiences. The annotated voter file and cross-tabulated results found in the scientific survey provide data from which to plan an effective communication strategy.

ELEMENT 8

Tasks and Timelines

Planning and executing a school tax election is, for most school leaders, one of the most complex and challenging leadership tasks they will encounter. A common reason for failure is lack of coordination between what the school district is doing and the activities of volunteers working in support of the election. Remember, if there isn't a written plan, it does not exist. Key campaign activities must be spelled out, coordinated, and scheduled on a day-to-day and week-to-week basis to ensure that no one drops the ball.

ELEMENT 9

Campaign Leadership

Merely *understanding* the need to involve a community in a grassroots effort falls well short of the target when it comes to successful tax elections. Your campaign can be well on its way toward a victory if you are strategic and focused on recruiting the "ideal task performer" for each and every leadership need. Do not send your campaign volunteers out into the community until they are thoroughly prepared and trained. And last, plan carefully for the appropriate role for the school board, administrators, staff, and community members.

ELEMENT 10
Campaign Execution

Pick your analogy—sports, ballet, business, or politics—they are one and the same. All of the research, planning, and training in the world will not matter if the school district, in cooperation with the campaign committee, cannot effectively execute the plan. The efforts of the school district and campaign committee must be driven by passion and an unrelenting commitment to success that is girded by high-quality execution from beginning to end.

Now, it's time to dive into the details. Each chapter builds upon the last as we provide school district leaders with sound advice about the planning and execution of school tax elections.

Chapter 1

Research to Practice

You thought you had done everything right. You devoured the research, interrogated winning superintendents from Albuquerque to Azusa, and replicated successful campaign strategies from neighboring school districts. But when the ballots were finally counted, you found yourself on the losing end of an important school tax election. What happened?

Since there is no pat formula for success, school leaders should roll up their sleeves, dig in, and become students of sound research and successful practice. In the final analysis, there is no better road map to a successful election. In fact, university libraries are replete with dissertations documenting that winning campaigns use research-based strategies to a *greater extent* and *more effectively* than unsuccessful ones. Understanding the research on school tax elections and thoughtfully implementing these strategies form the foundation of a successful campaign.

To begin with, it is important to avoid a potentially shortsighted focus on campaign tactics and instead strive for a more comprehensive understanding of the research related to school tax elections. Without a basic understanding of the research-based variables most often associated with success, school leaders can easily slip into a frantic strategy of piecing together a hodgepodge of tactics from the archives of successful elections. Distributing the top ten reasons to vote "yes" inside fortune cookies might have been a hit in a neighboring district, but this tactic could bomb in your community unless done within the context of a comprehensive, research-based election plan. School leaders need to understand that broad campaign strategies and the specific tactics to achieve them must be built upon and flow from a strong foundation of election research.

The research of Philip Piele and John Hall, completed nearly fifty years ago, still provides the base for many contemporary dissertations and scholarly works on this topic. *Budgets, Bonds, and Ballots* (1973) summarizes

1

more than a decade of research by analyzing and categorizing 61 election variables. Research studies for each of the variables are labeled as being significantly positive, negative, or at least statistically related to the results of these elections. Their research summary emphasizes the difference between contextual variables (e.g., wealth) that are generally out of the practitioner's control and specific campaign strategies selected by a school leader.

Understanding and applying election research within the unique context of a school community is part of the art of leadership within this framework. The campaign plan then becomes a carefully woven fabric of strategies designed to interact with and influence the environment within the school district. Dozens of other authors build on Piele and Hall's "megastudy," carrying the research forward into the present day. In the course of writing this book, we revisited the foundations of election research through more contemporary studies.

What have we learned about school elections over the decades? In our experience, the following eleven factors are most often associated, in both research and practice, with successful school tax elections. In combination, they form the foundation for our planning model.

FACTOR 1
Unanimous Election Resolution and Support by School Board throughout Campaign

School board solidarity is one of 20 variables examined by Piele and Hall (1973), with all studies pointing to a positive correlation between unanimity and successful elections. T. N. Pullium (1983) asserts that "total support by members of the school board is almost always necessary for the success of a school referendum" (p. 50). Another researcher more bluntly warns, "A school board whose members have not reached a consensus on the content and format of the referendum should not embark on a campaign" (Etheredge, 1989, p. 46). Blount (1991), Dunbar (1991), Brummer (1999), Mobley (2007), and Kraus (2009) cite similar findings. Clearly, this is a critical factor demanding attention long before a proposal is placed on the school board agenda. While elections have been won with less than unanimous boards, the amount of extra work and distraction this causes is something to be avoided if at all possible.

High Levels of Community Trust, Satisfaction, and Perceptions of Quality for Local Public Schools

School districts would be well advised to borrow from the Ford Motor Company tagline and "make quality Job 1." Lifto and Morris (2000) focus on the quality question in their evaluation of 107 Minnesota school tax elections between 1996 and 2000. The common variable in each of the campaigns was preelection polling during which they asked, "How would you rate the quality of education in your public schools—excellent, good, only fair, or poor?"

How important is quality in relationship to school tax elections? In this study, 96 percent of the cases revealed that the size of the negative evaluation (i.e., fair or poor) discriminated between winning and losing campaigns. When more than 17 percent of the public gave their public schools fair or poor marks, 27 out of 30 elections failed. By comparison, when less than 17 percent rated their schools as fair or poor, 76 out of 77 elections passed.[1] Maintaining a core value of quality as Job 1 is essential because "success at the polls is substantially driven by how your community views the quality of its public schools" (Lifto & Morris, 2000, p. 17). Studies by Corrick (1995), Phillips (1995), Williamson (1997), Schrom (2004), Faltys (2006), Godown (2011), Wheatley (2012), and Hoh (2017) echo the importance of residents' perceptions of accountability, quality, and continuous improvement.

Comprehensive Campaign Planning and Effective Execution Based on Current Research, Best Practices, and Demographic Characteristics of the Community

The ability to understand and effectively apply election research in a particular context is critical and positively correlates with success. More than three decades of research emphasize the importance of comprehensive planning and use of research-based strategies. Piele and Hall (1973), acting as pragmatists, remind school leaders that using research, conducting comprehensive planning, and then executing a world-class campaign are all within the control of the practitioner and *do* matter. J. F. Henderson Jr.'s (1986) study of Colorado school elections matches election outcomes with use of nine key campaign strategies. The more these factors were used the more likely the election was successful. Underscoring that a cookie cutter approach does not work, Williamson (1997) concludes that school districts are more successful when research and campaign strategies are adapted to the community's values and demographic characteristics. Similar findings are presented by Meszaros (2010), Godown (2011), Sargent (2014), Werner (2012), Morris (2016), and Kreimer (2017).

FACTOR 4

Outstanding Public Relations throughout the Year, Tailored to Unique Audiences within the District and Focused on the Purpose, Benefits, and Consequences of a Successful or Unsuccessful Election

Serving as a foundation for successful tax elections, the quality of public engagement and related communication strategies is evident throughout the research. The most successful districts achieve three key attributes when it comes to public relations:

- Outstanding quality;
- Ongoing public relations; and
- Focused messages to different audiences emphasizing the proposal's purpose and benefits.

One researcher highlighted the need for ongoing engagement by warning campaigners not to "commit the fatal error [of] trying to educate the electorate while at the same time urging school supporters to vote" (Etheredge, 1989, p. 34). As the percentage of registered voters with children who are public school students continues to decrease, it is also important to develop the capacity to communicate multiple messages to a number of audiences. A multitude of researchers, including Lode (1999), Hinson (2001), Neill (2003), Clemens (2003), Kraus (2009), Lifto and Senden (2010), and Sargent (2014), join the choir, emphasizing similar conclusions.

The Use of Scientific Polling to Better Understand the Community's Perceptions, Understanding, and Readiness for Proposal

Designing and administering a scientific poll drawn from the school district's registered voter file is one of the most important preelection activities and positively correlates with success. In addition to studying the community's understanding and support for the district's proposal, surveys also provide the opportunity to benchmark key community perceptions (e.g., overall quality or financial management), some of which are linked with success and all of which will help target effective communications to key audiences. Basing decisions on reliable survey data is a potent political strategy closely tied to winning elections and integral to effective campaign communication. Sullivan (1993), Dalton (1995), Henderson (1986), and Moore (2018) each authored studies that connect a school district's understanding of the community's attitudes and perceptions via scientific surveys with election day success.

Strong Alignment between the Proposal's Purpose and Cost and the Community's Priorities and Willingness to Pay Higher Taxes

School leaders must determine how to align the ballot question with what the community wants because "each district has its own collective demand for education under varying tax cost conditions" (Sclafani, 1985, p. 25). When it comes to school tax elections, alignment has two dimensions: the "what," or content of the proposal, and the "how much," or the cost and tax impact. A campaign supporting the district has an advantage when the ballot question is congruent on both counts, aligning the values of the community *with* its collective willingness to pay in the form of higher property taxes. Dalton (1995), Galton (1996), Brummer (1999), Hinson (2001), Friedland (2002), Clemens (2003), and Packer (2013) document similar results.

FACTOR 7
Broad-Based Strategic Community Involvement in Planning and Executing a Campaign

Although "flying under the radar" may be an appealing approach in some communities, the preponderance of evidence suggests that broad, strategic community involvement is paramount to success in most circumstances. Few communities enjoy the luxury of having public school children in more than one-third of their households. As a result, if a district expects to garner enough support to win the election, significant community involvement is usually the only option. It is important to note that community involvement has important quantitative *and* qualitative dimensions. Elections are more successful when the ideal task performers are recruited for specific campaign functions. Henderson (1997), Brummer (1999), Lode (1999), Friedland (2002), Pappalardo (2005), Geurink (2008), Russo (2010), Godown (2011), and Stauffacher (2012) are just a few of the many researchers who have positively correlated broad community involvement with successful elections.

FACTOR 8
Effective Use of Voter File and Other Demographic and Predictive Databases to Target, Canvass, and Deliver "Yes" Voters to the Polls

One of the challenges facing school leaders during a school tax election is to "remember that a referendum is a political—not an education—campaign" (Etheredge, 1989, p. 39). Grassroots committees seeking to elect candidates to local, state, and national office have long relied on registered voter files as the backbone of effective campaign work. The voter history files, parent files, and past-supporter archives provide key data for voter targeting, focused communications, and get-out-the-vote efforts. Drawing the random sample for the survey from the voter history file allows the campaign to link key survey findings with particular blocs of citizens in the voter file and their likelihood of voting in the school tax election. Quantitative and qualitative studies by researchers such as True (1996), Williamson (1997), Lode (1999), Kinsall (2000), Pappalardo

(2005), Lifto and Senden (2015), and Kobren (2015) support the use of data to target, canvass, and effectively get the "yes" voters to the polls.

FACTOR 9

Success in Obtaining Key VIP
and Organizational Endorsements

"The personal influence of influentials (opinion leaders) may be a critical factor in legitimizing (making acceptable) school proposals among voters" (Kimbrough & Nunnery, 1971, pp. 50–54). Identifying and engaging the power structure within a community can be a significant factor in determining an election's outcome. Doing so can be easier in smaller, more stable communities versus sprawling suburbs, where influence is more diffused. Endorsements from the media and key organizations can also be very helpful in building a base of community support. Developing relationships with these individuals and groups should be an important ongoing component of community engagement strategies. True (1996) and Stockton (1996) cite the positive influence of endorsements.

FACTOR 10

Absence of Community Conflict
and Avoidance of Organized Opposition

Significant community conflict and the organized opposition it often yields are difficult to overcome even with the best of campaigns. The distraction of conflict is bad enough, but even worse is that "citizens stimulated to vote by this community conflict have a tendency to cast negative ballots" (Chandler, 1989, pp. 21–22). Although it is impossible to control this variable completely, school leaders can use two strategies to minimize the damage. First, while "it may be impossible to eliminate tax resistance, . . . it can be controlled by attempting to reduce other controversies" (Allen, 1985, p. 94). For example, if your district needs to redo elementary boundaries, perhaps it can wait until after the election. School leaders should also attempt to "negotiate positions between influentials . . . so that the needs of education and children are not held hostage by two warring factions" (Kimbrough & Nunnery, 1971, pp. 22–23). Galton (1996), Day (1996), Franklin (1997), Friedland (2002), Mobley (2007), and Stauffacher (2012) authored other studies documenting the effect of conflict and organized opposition.

FACTOR 11
Funding for Technology
and Safety Enhancements

For the community that may be more self-centered and less egalitarian than in the past, communicating site-specific improvements is increasingly important. Many voters will be influenced by how the proposed improvements will affect *their* children or *their* neighborhood school. The almost universal desire for a school district to remain technologically advanced can also be a key factor. In a study of Oklahoma bond campaigns, Beckham (2001) found that elections were six times more likely to pass if they included an investment in technology. The higher the investment, the more likely the election would pass. Other researchers, including Williamson (1997) and Hockersmith (2001), drew parallel conclusions.

Part of the new normal for school districts relates to increasing the number of school tax elections that seek additional funding for enhancements to school safety, fueled by the relentless and heartbreaking onslaught of school shootings. These safety investments take the form of remodeled school entryways as well as sophisticated electronic surveillance equipment. To illustrate the demand for these types of investments moving forward, consider the following data from SchoolBondFinder:

• In 2015, 91 projects were financed with issuance of bonds to pay for technology and infrastructure related to alarms or surveillance equipment.
• In 2018, the number of similar projects jumped more than sixfold, from 91 to 608.

While this represents an impressive increase in a relatively short period of time, the most recent count at 608 underestimates the actual number of safety projects because school district bonding sometimes includes money for these types of projects without mentioning them specifically in the bond records. In addition, similar projects can be funded with revenue sources other than bonds. Data is from SchoolBondFinder.com.

The good news related to what will be a steadily growing investment in school safety projects can be found in prereferendum survey results. In dozens of scientific, random-sample surveys done to measure the feasibility of these tax proposals, funding for these types of safety upgrades has consistently tested strongly across a broad range of demographic groups.

Research matters, regardless of whether it is quantitative studies and chi-square tests or qualitative studies and triangulation. Hundreds of studies have been done since the publication of *Budgets, Bonds, and Ballots* (1973) against a backdrop of tens of thousands of school tax elections. This adds up to a substantial body of research and successful practice from which to draw. It is incumbent upon school leaders to build their election planning on this foundation and develop research-based strategies customized for their unique contexts. By doing so, more school districts will be successful on election day, and more students will have their educational needs met in our nation's public schools.

Note

1. The null hypothesis—that quality had nothing to do with election success or failure—was rejected at the 0.005 level.

Chapter 2

Voter File and Target Structure[1]

In 1970, Chicago's classic hit "25 or 6 to 4" spent twenty weeks on Billboard's Top 20, later becoming a favorite for school marching bands from Maine to California. While twenty weeks is impressive given the legendary rock 'n' roll acts performing back then, it pales in comparison to how many times over the years the group's leader, Robert Lamm, was asked to explain the meaning of his lyrics. Speculation ranged from a secret code for LSD to a rhetorical response to a question posed in the title of another recording—"Does Anybody Know What Time It Is?" Lamm clarified the actual meaning of "25 or 6 to 4" much later, but that's for you to Google if you are curious.

So what does "25 or 6 to 4" have to do with voter files, target structures, and the numbers driving the outcomes of school tax referendums? The short answer is that, not unlike Chicago's lyrical puzzle, school tax referendums have their own numbers represented by "15 or 20 to 25." Understanding the meaning and impact of these numbers is crucial within the broader context of composing and executing a successful tax election. The significance of "15 or 20 to 25" can be linked to three words—scarcity, absence, and opposition. These three factors can be quantified in an annotated voter file and then reflected in the campaign's target structure.

Demographics of Scarcity:
15 to 25 Percent

Registered voter data is one of the bedrocks of partisan politics. Long ago, a campaign recorded this information on index cards and stored them in a cardboard box, whereas today the collection of registered voter data is driven by technology and sophisticated databases. How many registered voters live in the jurisdiction that will elect the next governor or decide whether to approve issuance of debt for a new school? How many are Democrats versus Republicans? What's the count by gender? Young versus old? How many voters can be counted upon to show up, and which ones will go to the polls only if drawn by the drama of presidential politics?

In planning school tax elections, the demographics of scarcity depicted by the 15 percent to 25 percent reference relates to the number of parents as a percentage of all registered voters. In most school districts, registered voters who do not have children enrolled in the local public schools outnumber parents by about a 4 to 1 margin—a daunting reality of scarcity. Fueling this demographic reality is the aging of the older population of voters—those voters who are sixty-five and older. In 2009, approximately 36.9 million older adults lived in the United States, which was about 13 percent of the US population. By 2030, the US Department of Health and Human Services estimates older adults will number about 72.1 million (agingstats.gov). Age demographics have significant implications for voter targeting and messaging related to school tax referendums.

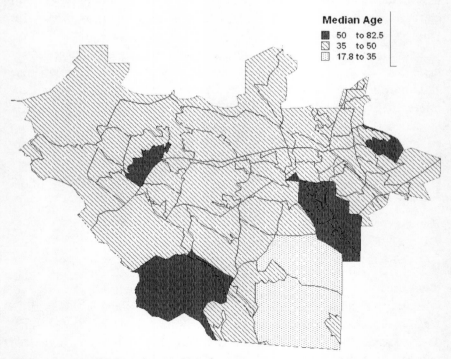

Figure 2.1   Distribution of Voters Based on Age

Demographics of Absence:
15 to 25 Percent

The demographics of absence, unfortunately, build on the first point, essentially creating a "double whammy" of scarcity. This further erodes what started as a proportionately small core base of natural supporters. In explaining absence in this context, the problem for school districts is both ironic and an inconvenient truth: Parents don't vote! To offset this reality, school districts must incorporate historical turnout patterns into the projections of likely "yes" votes from the parent base while implementing strategies to counter this unwanted pattern.

A postelection analysis (PEA) is a valuable analytical tool to use after a school tax election (win or lose). This analysis quantifies the participation (and conversely the absence) of key demographic groups (including parents) within the school district (see chapter 3, "Looking Back to Plan Forward").

Demographics of Opposition:
15 to 25 Percent

"Read my lips—no!" would be both accurate and more colorful in characterizing the meaning of demographics of opposition. In hundreds of scientific, random-sample feasibility surveys, one of the probes commonly used in phone interviews asks respondents to react to a statement: "I would not vote for a tax increase of any kind, in any amount no matter what the money was used for." Voters are presented with a five-point Likert scale ranging from "strongly agree" to "strongly disagree." In this context, the 15 percent to 25 percent range comes into play again, representing the typical range of voters who agree with the statement. Taking the midpoint of this range, one in five voters is basically in the "lost cause" column before the first note is played at the campaign's kickoff rally.

Oppositional forces—whether in the form of a paid "vote no" consultant, one individual on a mission, a loosely affiliated group of voters opposed to the school district's proposal, or a highly organized and funded "vote no" campaign—present significant challenges for successful school tax elections. It is incumbent upon school leaders to thoughtfully evaluate the likelihood and strength of potential opposition and harness research and best practices to blunt the damage to the campaign. And again, a fully annotated voter file with demographic markers is key to planning and responding effectively.

Unless your school district is an exception—and there aren't many—the campaign plan will need to develop multiple strategies to blunt the reality of starting behind on all three aspects of scarcity. At the same time, the campaign must include strategies for mining enough "yes" voters from other demographic groups within the school community.

Developing Strategies

Understanding the numbers and their implications for school tax elections is the first step in preparing for a successful school tax election. Like the music fans of Chicago in the 1970s, understanding the significance of "15 or 20 to 25" is important in this preparation. Like the index cards of yesteryear, it is incumbent on school leaders to prepare the voter file and target structure analytics to more accurately quantify the demographics of scarcity, absence, and opposition. If your district is not an exception, you should assume the campaign will need to grapple with these demographic realities and implement strategies to grow the base of "yes" voters from other targeted groups within the community. Fortunately, technology and access to sophisticated demographic and predictive databases provide new and better ways to uncover unknown or underutilized pockets of support.

Building a Voter File

Like Biff in *Back to the Future II*, we have all had the fantasy that we can see the future and make a killing by either buying the right lottery ticket or betting on the right team. While it's impossible to develop a clear view of the future by traveling through time, school tax elections have access to resources that offer a clearer picture of the future and a foundation for planning. The first of these tools—one that dramatically increases the value of all other campaign tools—is a fully annotated voter file.

Developing a voter file and subsequent target structure begins with acquiring a database of registered voters living within district boundaries. The availability and acceptable use of these data vary based on state law. In most states, a registered voter file can be acquired for election planning or research from a county or a state agency overseeing elections. While obtaining voter data from a county or state source has been the best option historically, there have been significant differences in ease of access, cost, and the content and quality of these databases. After researching alternatives, we discontinued accessing voter data from government sources in 2018 and now obtain needed voter data from L2, a Washington-based commercial vendor (L2political.com).

L2 provides registered voter data, including dozens of demographic characteristics of the registered voters living within a school district. Demographic markers include age, gender, housing type (rent vs. own), level of education attained, household income, location within the jurisdiction (e.g., community, precinct, or municipality), race/ethnicity, and parental status. All of these markers combine to build a foundation for a school tax election. The graphic below (figure 2.2) depicts annotating additional demographic and predictive databases with the L2 registered voter file. The resulting spreadsheet file provides rich sorting capabilities for different phases of the campaign.

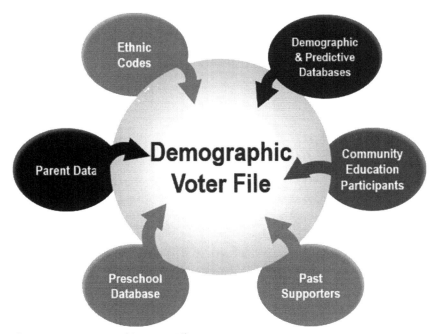

Figure 2.2 Demographic Voter File

Demographic Databases

In addition to the demographic markers contained within the L2 voter file package, school campaigns can access a variety of other commercial databases that provide enhanced demographic information that can be annotated to the registered voter file. One example we have used in both random-sample feasibility surveys and voter identification and get-out-the-vote campaign execution is PRIZM Premier. This commercial database combines demographic, consumer behavior, and geographic data to help identify and engage with groups of voters based on their membership in one of 68 demographic and behavioral segments. When used in conjunction with a feasibility survey, PRIZM Premier helps identify which of the 68 segments of voters are most supportive of (or most opposed to) the specific referendum proposal both in terms of content of the ballot question and cost. For more information about PRIZM Premier by Claritas, LLC, visit MyBestSegments.com.

Predictive Databases

Predictive analytics propel voter file annotations to a new level, fueled by technology that dissects and analyzes dozens of demographic, lifestyle, and consumer characteristics. School districts can identify and quantify groups of registered voters who are more likely to support school tax proposals. These commercial databases can also predict the likelihood of each resident casting a ballot based on past voting behaviors. Three examples of predictive databases available to campaigns are:

- Haystaq DNA (haystaqdna.com);
- Mosaic USA (segmentationportal.com/us); and
- NGP VAN or Voter Activation Network (ngpvan.com).

At the time of this writing, we have primarily used NGP VAN to further enhance a voter file and target structure.

The VAN predictive database assigns each registered voter a numerical score of 1 to 100, based on its predictive analytical model. The higher the score, the more likely a group of voters will support a progressive

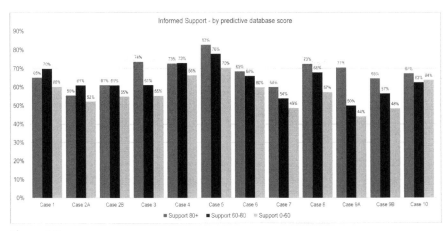

Figure 2.3

proposal. When we have accessed VAN numbers to further enhance a voter file for a school district we focused on voters with assigned VAN scores of 80 or higher. In cases in which we have completed a scientific, random-sample phone survey to test support for a school tax election, incorporating the VAN scores has allowed us to quantify and evaluate to what extent voters with higher VAN scores supported (or opposed) specific ballot proposals. Figure 2.3 includes data from 10 referenda conducted in 2017 and 2018. Support from voters with VAN scores of 80–100 averaged 11 percent higher than support from voters with VAN scores of 60–80.

Target Structure

Building an annotated file of registered voters—enhanced with rich data from demographic and/or predictive databases—provides the school district and the campaign with the ability to build a target structure for a future school tax election. Suppose, for example, a district has 30,000 registered voters and based on past turnout history expects a turnout of 40 percent in an upcoming school tax election. Assuming the district is in a simple majority state to win (i.e., 50 percent +1), it will take 15,001 "yes" votes to win on election day. A target structure essentially is looking for what Haustaq DNA would characterize as the "needles in the haystack." In other words, from the overall database of 30,000 registered voters, what specific voters are more likely to support a proposal and actually cast a ballot?

A target structure identifies these voters and sorts them into piles from most supportive and most likely to vote to least supportive and least likely to vote. Target A will represent the best set of voters based on these two characteristics, and Target F will represent the worst. Assigning voters to theses concentric targets is accomplished through use of the demographic and predictive databases, and in our experience, further enhanced by analyzing results of a well-designed, scientific, random-sample survey testing support for the ballot proposal across demographic characteristics in the voter file. Below is a graphical example of such a target structure depicting expected levels of support, the likelihood of voting based on past voting behavior, and the size of each target group. These targets can be sorted by name, address, and phone numbers for executing key phases of the campaign.

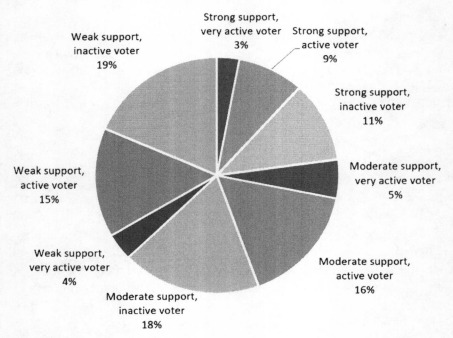

Figure 2.4
Target Structure of Registered Voters Based on Support and Likelihood to Vote

The preparation of an annotated voter file is presented early in our discussion to emphasize its foundational importance. It is the key planning tool for the "Big 3" in successful school tax elections: canvassing, communications, and get-out-the-vote. Beginning with a database of all registered voters and then enhancing that file with relevant demographic and predictive markers to the file, the district and campaign have the data to drive and inform the effort to pass the next ballot proposal.

Note

1. Portions of this chapter originally appeared in "By the Numbers: A School District's Tax Elections," Don E. Lifto, PhD, published in *The School Administrator*, American Association of School Administrators, December 2017.

Chapter 3

Looking Back to Plan Forward[1]

In promoting its former primetime hit *Crossing Jordan*, NBC touted co-star Jill Hennessy as "a sexy, smart, and fearless Boston medical examiner with a penchant for going beyond the call of duty to investigate crimes." A large fan base of forensic groupies tuned in weekly to watch Jordan "channel her inner anger toward piecing together complex murder cases that have been hidden, shoved aside—or conveniently forgotten," as the network put it. Rival CBS followed with another forensic blockbuster in *CSI: Crime Scene Investigation*. In both cases, solving crimes required that clues first be coaxed from the dead and reassembled to understand what actually happened. Albeit not as sexy, school leaders also must be smart and fearless as they conduct their forensic studies at the examination table of school tax elections past.

Research and practice have yet to yield a modus operandi in K–12 education that always produces winners on school tax proposals. Whether it's construction and renovation or requests for more operating money, each election type and context are unique, with no guarantee that a set of campaign strategies—even if previously successful in another district—won't fail in your community. If successful campaigns were not such a delicate balance of science and art, the formula for success would have long since been discovered, resulting in significantly more school districts finding success at the polls. This reality aside, both research and successful practice suggest the best way to start planning your next successful facility or operating referendum is to take a much closer look at your last.

The idea that a school district should look back at its last election when planning the next election is based on the concept that one of the best predictors of future voting behavior is the past actions of those voters. Therefore, understanding the key factors and behaviors in past local elections will help a district plan a successful election in the future.

Rearview Mirror

Many school districts squander a key strategic opportunity when they fail to collect, analyze, and archive valuable data after a school tax referendum—regardless of the campaign's outcome. The most obvious data analysis, although often not done well, is to understand who participated in a recent school referendum in comparison to earlier elections. How did the campaign effort in support of the ballot question influence the electorate? How did various demographic groups vote relative to their proportionate share of the voter file as well as past voting habits? To what extent did targeted supporters show up from various precincts or attendance areas? These are examples of the questions that can be answered by doing a postelection analysis, yielding critical information for school leaders who are planning future campaigns.

LESSONS FROM THE PAST

There are basic questions that need to be asked during a postelection analysis. The answers to these questions form the "lesson" for planners of your next election.

- What type of election just occurred?
- When might this type of election occur again?
- Did parents participate in this school tax referendum?
- If parent participation was not uniform, are there parent groups that will need a little extra attention during the next election?
- Did identified nonparent supporters participate?
- What can the next campaign learn from the participation of nonparent supporters?
- Are there areas of the district that present unique challenges to the next campaign? The characteristics of these areas and the attitudes of the voters who live in them should be explored with maps and surveys.

Before digging more deeply into turnout and support levels based on demography and the campaign's target structure, a first step is to explore at the macro level geographic differences within the school district focusing on turnout percentages and levels of support. These geographic dif-

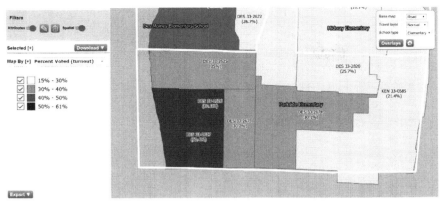

Figure 3.1   Turnout Percentage by Attendance Area
Source: GuideK12

ferences can be analyzed based on precincts, school attendance areas, or other natural boundaries. Comparing and contrasting turnout and level of support percentages can sometimes reveal key outcomes that need to be addressed in your next tax election.

For example, the voting precinct with the highest level of support for the ballot measure might have also had the lowest turnout percentage—clearly a strategic issue that needs attention before the next tax election. Building a solid understanding of these interactions can be enhanced with use of geovisual mapping, as reflected in the two examples below. Figure 3.1 depicts turnout percentages, and figure 3.2 depicts the percentage of "yes" votes cast in the referendum.

Figure 3.2   Support Level by Attendance Area
Source: GuideK12

After looking at turnout and levels of support in different parts of the district, the next step is to isolate all voter file information about the population who voted in the district's most recent election. Once these populations are isolated, their demographic characteristics are counted and compared to the population of all voters in the district. Specifically, we want to know which demographic groups are overrepresented or underrepresented in this population.

For example, the counts developed to identify the number of male and female voters who cast ballots are used to calculate the percentage of the total number of participating voters who are male versus female. These percentages are then compared to the entire voter file. This process is repeated for each significant demographic feature. A typical result might show that although women make up 52 percent of all registered voters in the district, postelection research finds women made up 56 percent of the population who voted. The district now knows its last election attracted more women than men.

Knowing the election attracted more women allows us to ask additional questions. Were these older or younger women? How many of these women have school-age children? Do these women have a long-term history of voting in every local election, or do they generally not vote? Each detail is a clue that allows us to create a picture of what happened on election day. That picture, in turn, serves as a road map for the district's next school tax referendum.

What about the men in the district? If men are underrepresented in the population who voted, we want to ask all of the same questions to determine the characteristics of male voters who missed this election. In one specific case, a postelection analysis found that a large number of the men who did not vote were younger parents with relatively weak voting histories. While their wives had gotten to the polls to vote for the district's proposal, these potential parent "yes" votes failed to cast a ballot. This information allowed the district to add a new element—a male mentor program to help remind fathers to vote—to its next campaign plan.

As part of the program, a team of older male parents with long-term voting records worked throughout the campaign to communicate directly with younger dads. At each step, they emphasized the need not only to support the school district's proposal as a volunteer but also to vote "yes" on election day. An analysis of the campaign results confirmed that it worked. Not only did turnout among younger male parents increase significantly, but the district also turned a heartbreaking loss into a solid win.

Once a profile of the voting population has been developed, a postelection analysis turns to look in detail at the election-day performance of two groups—those who were identified as supporters of the district's proposal among all registered voters and those who were identified among parents. Each group needs to be examined in two ways:

- How was each group represented on election day?
- Did most of the people in each group cast a ballot?

In both groups, overrepresentation is extremely important. For example, if parents represent 23 percent of the registered voter population, they are overrepresented if we find they comprised 36 percent of the population who voted on election day. In all cases, we want to find parents overrepresented in school tax elections. This is the result of two factors that exist in almost every school tax election. First, parents should naturally be attracted to a school tax election. Second, every school tax referendum must have a campaign plan designed to maximize the parent vote.

Therefore, if parents are underrepresented in the population who voted on election day, either there was a serious flaw in the planning and/or execution of the campaign or the district's proposal was significantly out of alignment with the priorities of the parent population. Any district that finds itself in this situation has some major work ahead—work that must be completed before considering another school tax referendum.

Even when parents are overrepresented in the population who voted, the district needs to look at the degree to which the potential vote within the parent population was maximized. For example, if parents represent 23 percent of the voter file but comprise 36 percent of the population who voted, an initial conclusion could be that parent participation in the election was strong. But, if only 43 percent of all registered parents took the time to cast a ballot, this initial conclusion would be wrong. Leaving 57 percent of the parent population at home on election day means the campaign failed to maximize the parent vote. Such a situation can easily spell the difference between a win and a loss.

Knowing that parent participation might be a problem allows the district's next effort to structure its campaign plan to address this challenge.

Where absentee or early voting is easy, campaigns often plan to guide all supportive parents with weak voting histories to the polls to vote early. Such campaigns may even include the preprinting of absentee ballot applications so recipients only need to sign the form and wait for their ballot to arrive in the mail. Other campaigns have developed extensive "buddy systems." Similar to the male mentor program, parents who can be counted on to vote are assigned a number of election buddies (i.e., parents without solid voting records). Throughout the campaign, these parents systematically contact their "buddies" to emphasize the importance of every vote.

USING A POSTMORTEM TO TARGET FUTURE VOTERS

The results of a postelection analysis often cause a district to modify the way in which voters are targeted in the next campaign. For example, a large school district placed a bond proposal on the ballot and then executed an extremely weak communications effort. As a result, the bond proposal failed to win voter support. In a postelection analysis, it became very clear that only one-third of the parent population had voted in this election. In their second effort, parents were divided into two target groups. Group 1 was made up of those parents who, despite a weak communications effort, found out that a bond was on the ballot and voted. Group 2 comprised those parents who did not vote in the first election. Instead of incurring the cost of increasing the amount of mail and telephone contact made with all parents, the second campaign was able to focus an increased amount of contact where it was needed most—on the parents in Group 2. This group of parents received two to three times as much mail as the first group and was the focus of more telephone contact by campaign volunteers. The result was a large increase in parent participation and a win on election day.

A postelection analysis also involves a careful look at the nonparent voters identified by the campaign as supporting the district's referendum proposal. Though many techniques can be used to identify supporters who are not parents, all rely on campaign volunteers asking community members if they will support the proposal. In successful campaigns, this is not a random contact program. Specific portions of the nonparent population are targeted for contact by the campaign. After election day, it is important to look at how well this population performed and, in turn, evaluate the effectiveness of the campaign's targeting effort. Are identified supporters overrepresented or underrepresented in the population who voted? What percentage of the total number of identified supporters cast ballots?

As with the parent population, identified supporters may be overrepresented in the population who voted, but the campaign may not be satisfied with the actual percentage casting ballots. Results can vary greatly. We have seen results ranging from a dismal 33 percent of supporters participating in the election up to an outstanding 95 percent of identified support casting ballots.

Especially when the potential in this population is not maximized, analysis provides the needed information to craft a more effective campaign plan. By looking at the gender, age, party affiliation, and geographic location of identified supporters, such an analysis will allow a campaign to develop a clear picture of the individuals who failed to cast ballots. For example, if such an analysis reveals that all younger identified supporters who were Democrats with a weak long-term voting record did not vote, this fact will help the next campaign target its volunteer resources more effectively.

Another example will help to emphasize this point. A number of campaigns have developed extensive plans to maximize the "yes" votes cast by recent school district graduates. These young voters are very often still registered in the community, although they may be living on a college campus, on a military base, or in an apartment. They can usually be identified in the voter file by combining their age with the fact that they are still associated with a parent household due to the presence of a younger sibling. These campaigns often work with these young adults during the summer or winter break to inform them of the importance of their vote in the district's upcoming election.

Parents are also reminded of the importance of helping ensure their recent graduates vote and are provided with information about how they can vote absentee if needed. This effort may also extend to social media in order to stay in touch even when these potential supporters are out of the district. A postelection analysis of the votes cast by these younger voters will determine if this campaign tactic works. When it does, it should be included in the next campaign. When it does not, it should be replaced with a more effective tactic.

Finally, a postelection analysis should examine how the election a district just held compares to other recent elections. Too many school districts make the assumption that all elections are alike. They are not. Each election has a character that is defined by the types of candidates or issues that appear on the ballot alongside the district's proposal as well as the year and month of the election.

For example, a November election for a governor or the president will attract a much younger, more male population than a primary, school board, or special election. The latter generally will attract a population that is older, more female, and more likely to vote in any election held in the area. Therefore, if your district just held a very successful school tax referendum on the same ballot as a high turnout presidential election, it should not be assumed that the same campaign plan can be applied to your next election, especially if it's being held on a special election ballot with a much lower turnout.

One of the biggest differences among elections is the level of turnout. Despite all the concern surrounding declining presidential election turnout during the past fifty years, a presidential election will attract the highest level of turnout in most communities, typically in the 60 to 75 percent range. An even-year, nonpresidential election will typically draw 50 to 65 percent of registered voters. There is generally a much lower level of voter participation in all other elections, such as nominating primary, city council, or school board elections, which are often in the 25 to 40 percent range. These election characteristics always need to be verified within your district. The number and types of voters anticipated must have a direct correlation with the actual number and types of voters to be successful.

A Tale of Two Votes

A facility referendum in the North Branch (Minnesota) Area Public Schools provides an excellent example of using a postelection analysis following a school tax election. On May 24, 2016, voters in the district went to the polls to cast ballots for or against a proposal to issue $62.1 million in new debt to fund various school district facilities projects. The projects included improving operating efficiency, safety and security, and traffic patterns as well as upgrades and remodeling to support instruction and improvements to facilities used for student activities and community events.

Although the district had lost ten of twelve referendum ballot questions since 1998, there was reason to be hopeful. The referendum was being held just as old debt was scheduled to retire, meaning the district could offer its taxpayers a building project with no tax increase. As the judges completed the ballot count, hopeful expectation was replaced with disappointment—the referendum had come up 125 votes short of the required 50 percent plus one needed for approval.

Building a Foundation

In the months that followed, North Branch Superintendent Deb Henton and the school board took stock of the situation and began a yearlong effort to analyze what had happened and begin the "brick-by-brick" building of a foundation capable of supporting a positive outcome in the future. The building needs were not going away, and the district needed to find a way to support students, staff, and the community. The good news was that the May referendum had failed by only 125 votes and the school board, administration, and citizens involved in the campaign were motivated to try again soon.

Demographics of Turnout and Opposition

Data from hundreds of scientific surveys testing the feasibility of school tax elections, as well as postelection analyses conducted over the same time period, reveal fairly consistent demographics of participation and opposition as discussed in chapter 2. Most districts land in the 15 to 25 percent range on three important demographic profiles. North Branch's postelection analysis confirmed the 15 to 25 percent reality in their failed 2016 referendum:

- Parents of school-age children attending the district accounted for only 23.4 percent of all registered voters.
- Turnout among young parents (eighteen to forty years old) came in at a meager 19.8 percent, with total parent turnout at only 27 percent.
- In polling after the 2016 defeat, but before the second try in May 2017, 21 percent of respondents agreed with the statement, "I would not vote for any tax increase of any amount for any purpose."

One year later, in May 2017, the district was equipped with better data from both a feasibility survey of voters who participated in the 2016 referendum and demographic results of a postelection analysis as well as the use of both demographic and predictive databases to develop a voter target structure for the campaign.

The school board ultimately broke up the proposal into three ballot questions totaling $70 million ($8 million more than in 2016). The district also used GuideK12, the geovisual mapping tool highlighted in chapter 4 ("Geovisual Demographic Mapping"), to map its voter targets to guide voter canvassing and get-out-the-vote efforts. Finally, the district developed a focused, research-based communications plan to guide its efforts. The district was rewarded for its strategic approach, winning all three ballot questions. While the demographics of the district did not change in a year, the turnout numbers were much better:

- Turnout among young parents (eighteen to forty years old) was 35.6 percent, a 79 percent improvement over the 2016 ballot defeat.
- Turnout among all parents was 39.4 percent, a 46 percent improvement over the previous year's defeat.
- The campaign achieved a turnout of 54.7 percent for its top two identified "yes" voter target groups, compared to a 24 percent turnout overall.
- The campaign targeted and turned out 759 early voters compared to only 122 in the failed election.

Planning Ahead by Looking Back

The purpose of looking back, of course, is to determine what happened and why. The foundation for success on election day begins with a postelection analysis that investigates what happened during prior district elections. Like the medical examiners in *Crossing Jordan* and *CSI*, successful school leaders need to piece together disconnected clues about voter behavior, demographic tendencies, and turnout under various conditions. Reconstructing this puzzle, in combination with other steps in a comprehensive planning model, provides the foundation for an effective campaign and guides the critical steps of voter identification and get-out-the-vote, which are key ingredients to achieving success in your next tax election.

Note

1. Portions of this chapter originally appeared in the January 2004 and December 2017 issues of *The School Administrator*. Copyright 2003 and 2017, American Association of School Administrators.

Chapter 4

Geovisual Demographic Mapping[1]

In his book, *Reflections*, author Idries Shah reflects on our current state of information and data overload. "People today are in danger of drowning in information," Shah laments. "But, because they have been taught that information is useful, they are more willing to drown than they need be. If they could handle information, they would not have to drown at all." Trying to manage and make sense of relevant data when planning and executing a school tax referendum has its dangers too—the very real threat of treading water in a swamp of Excel files and disparate demographic and predictive databases. It can be like trying to track down a criminal in TV's *Cold Case Files* or one of the many *CSI* or *Law and Order* clones.

Like a crime show, there is a problem to solve (in this case passing a school tax referendum), a trail of clues (the data), and the need to sink or swim in terms of how you effectively connect the data dots for use in your campaign. If a picture is truly worth a thousand words, a good set of demographic maps is worth thousands of columns of numbers, counts, and statistics. Simply put, the statistics defining a school district can be made much easier to read and understand when they are visually displayed in a set of demographic maps.

As part of the school tax referendum planning process, mapping attributes of voters can include characteristics such as their registration status, presence of school-age children, likelihood to vote in the next referendum based on historical voting patterns, market value of homes in a neighborhood or school attendance area, and differentiation of voters based on an established target structure. In this context, voters in target A would have been identified—based on a scientific, random-sample survey; a predictive data base; and/or canvassing—as those voters most likely to show up and cast a "yes" vote. Each subsequent target group after target A would

not be quite as strong in those two attributes as the target group that pre-
ceded it in the target hierarchy.

An effective GIS platform allows school leaders to *see and understand*
the meaning and implications of the data relevant to the referendum. The
platform connects myriad data sources into an interactive map, chart, or
graph that supports the three key functions of a successful school tax
campaign: voter canvassing, communications, and get-out-the-vote. Effective use of mapping tools decreases the likelihood of Shah's analogy
of drowning in spreadsheets and makes it easier to design and execute a
winning campaign. In this chapter, we will provide a brief overview of
how GIS mapping for school districts has developed, different types of
maps that can be used in support of school tax referendums, and specific
examples of GuideK12's mapping features.

Geovisual Mapping
Past to Present

School districts have had maps in their decision-making toolkits as long
as there have been schools offering transportation and school boundaries.
What has changed is how the maps are created and analyzed as well as the
decisions they can help administrators tackle within the context of broad,
ongoing planning over time. Early generations of maps were hand drawn,
and details or decisions were done by adding pins or strings to show
routes, change boundaries, or track areas under development. Superintendents in the 1980s used a corkboard with a map, yarn, and pins to plan bus
routes within district boundaries. Maps were typically housed and owned
by the transportation department. Over the years, despite exceptions
related to special projects, such as boundary changes, very few people
possessed a broad visual perspective of an individual school district. Fortunately, for school leaders responsible for planning and executing school
tax elections, that has changed.

With the advent of GPS and tools such as Google Maps, we have all
become accustomed to accessing maps with significant details at a touch of
a button. Geovisual analytics as a discipline is not new. Oil companies and
other industries where location is critical to their business have relied on the
ability to map data sets for guiding key decisions. Yet it has only been in
recent years that geovisual analytics have emerged in the education world.

School districts can now zoom down to individual student data at the
parcel level, and each student becomes a live point on the map. Multiple

dots are displayed for a multifamily dwelling. The ability to display real-time student data merged with other data sets (e.g., voter history) on an interactive map for strategic planning purposes opens a world of possibilities for school districts. Progressive districts must understand the available tools as well as the types of data and data sources in order to make data-driven decisions.

Geovisual Mapping Platforms

GIS software has also been around for a long time, but it is a complex tool requiring years of training to be proficient. Many districts have a transportation or planning department staff member who is trained in GIS software, but too often that can be an information bottleneck. Understanding the geographic context of your district's data is fundamental for making more informed decisions.

GuideK12, which is one geovisual mapping tool, is unique in at least two respects. First, it was designed exclusively for school district needs and enables busy administrators to quickly get the answers they need. This can be accomplished with minimal training, so you don't need a GIS expert on board to benefit from the mapping tool. Second, it is the only geovisual mapping platform with a referendum planning module. Information about GuideK12 and the four interactive modules within its analytics suite (figure 4.1) can be reviewed at https://guidek12.com/.

Within GuideK12's broad platform is its referendum planning tool found in the Explorer module. The screen shots below highlight some of the data that can be displayed to support key campaign activities by the district and advocacy committee. These data include identification of homesteaded versus nonhomesteaded properties, rental units, and estimated market value of these properties, again all mapped to the rooftop. In addition, GuideK12 is loaded with both parent data (i.e., parents of school-age children living within the district) and registered voter data. Explorer's quick and easy sorting can produce referendum maps useful to different phases of the campaign. For example, school leaders might want to see a map of parents but differentiated between parents who are registered to vote and those who are not. Or they might want a map of parents who are registered voters but unlikely participants in an upcoming school tax election based on their voting record in past elections.

Campaign targets can also be delineated based on the analysis of a random-sample survey and/or use of demographic or predictive databases

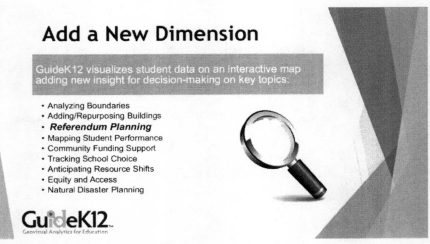

Add a New Dimension

GuideK12 visualizes student data on an interactive map adding new insight for decision-making on key topics.

- Analyzing Boundaries
- Adding/Repurposing Buildings
- *Referendum Planning*
- Mapping Student Performance
- Community Funding Support
- Tracking School Choice
- Anticipating Resource Shifts
- Equity and Access
- Natural Disaster Planning

GuideK12™
Geovisual Analytics for Education

Figure 4.1   GuideK12 Analytic Suite

(see chapter 2, "Voter File and Target Structure"). In this context, target A would be populated with registered voters identified as most likely to support the district's tax election and to show up and cast a ballot based on past voting behavior. All registered voters (including parents) would be populated into this target structure, typically organized in six concentric categories (targets A through F). Each subsequent target group after target A would be a comparatively weaker target for the tax election based on both expected level of support and turnout potential.

GuideK12's Explorer tools allow school leaders to sort in detail based on the specific needs of the district or campaign related to communications, including printing mailing labels based on specific targets of interest to the campaign. Mapping data can be used to geographically plan and organize door-to-door campaigning or get-out-the-vote. GuideK12 can also be used to designate specific walking zones if a campaign plan includes door knocking. Within these walking zones, the district can depict in detail the specific registered voters who are targeted for a door knock (figures 4.2 through 4.5). These targets can also be uploaded into a district's autodial platform for communications and get-out-the-vote reminders.

The ability to visualize the location of registered voters, parents in the district, or other high-potential "yes" voters has become a game-changing approach for referendums. Many districts forget that about only 25 percent of their community may have a child attending a district school and busy parents often have the best intentions but don't get to the polls on election day.

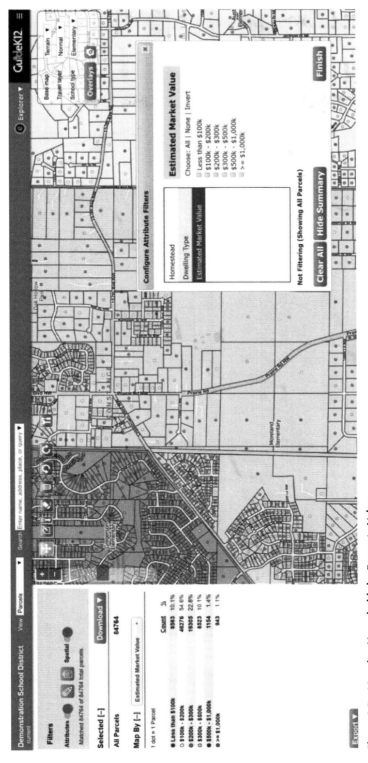

Figure 4.2   Mapping Households by Property Value

Source: GuideK12

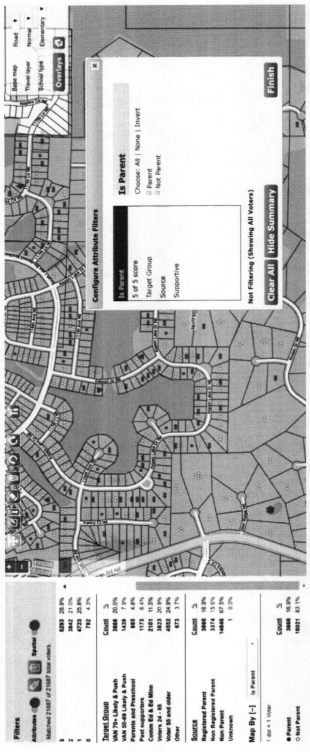

Figure 4.3 Mapping Voters by Target Structure
Source: GuideK12

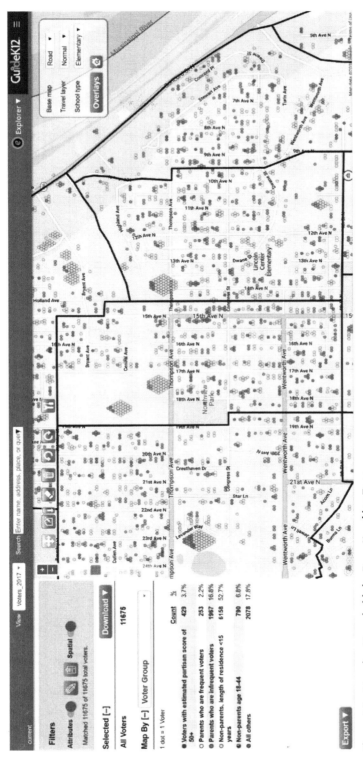

Figure 4.4 Mapping Households by Door-Knocking Zone

Source: GuideK12

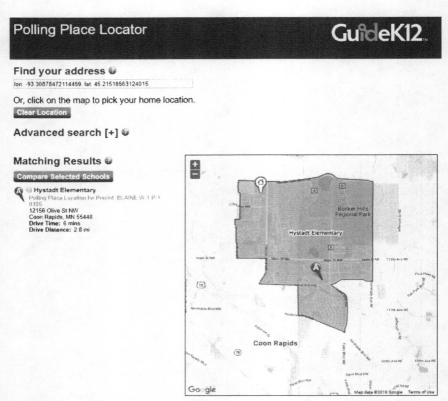

Figure 4.5   Mapping by Voters' Polling Sites
Source: GuideK12

Targeted campaigns with customized messaging are possible for mail-ings or door-knocking campaigns when volunteers know which doors to knock on and have a good sense of the reception they will get on the other side. Understanding the community of voters with better granularity allows the message to be customized. GuideK12's referendum-planning resources available in its Explorer suite have provided school districts with highly effective geovisual planning tools in support of a school tax election campaign.

If your district does not subscribe to GuideK12 or you want to expand upon the geovisual mapping available in GuideK12, the best resource is to access the US Census[2] Interactive Maps. Its mapping tools integrate avail-able census data with geographic boundary data and then create mapping tools to visualize data. Examples are illustrated here, mapping past vot-ing behavior and household income (figures 4.6 and 4.7), both of which could be relevant to a tax election when targeting messages, soliciting

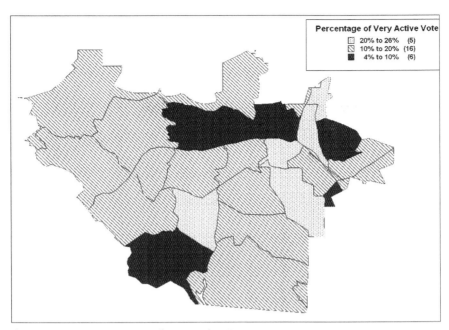

Figure 4.6   US Census Map of Past Voting Frequency

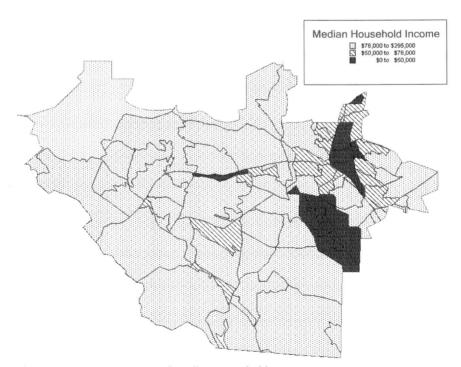

Figure 4.7   US Census Map of Median Household Income

contributions, or getting out the vote. US Census maps of these kinds can be accessed to support campaign planning and execution with minimal technical expertise.

Notes

1. Portions of this chapter originally appeared in "The Case of Precinct 5," Don E. Lifto, PhD, and J. Bradford Senden, PhD, published in *American School Board Journal*, NSBA, April 2005.

2. Information about how to access the US Census can be found at https://www.census.gov/geography/interactive-maps.html.

Chapter 5

Community Survey
Testing Feasibility[1]

A community survey is an important analytical tool to test the feasibility of a school tax election ballot proposal. In determining feasibility, a good survey evaluates and defines at least two key aspects of alignment: the content, or "what," of the ballot proposal and the cost, or "how much," in terms of the tax increase on various types of property within the school district. The preponderance of research attests to the fact that, when a ballot proposal is in sync with both aspects of alignment—the "what" and "how much" of a school tax referendum—the district has a better chance of success on election day.

The methodologies used for a community survey—fueled by more sophisticated technology and software in recent years—are increasingly varied in approach. Like all professions, the challenge to select from an expanding array of survey approaches can be complicated by the terminology used to describe them. In making these decisions, school leaders should choose a methodology that will provide reasonably accurate feasibility testing of a school tax proposal while remaining cost effective to administer. This chapter will assist school leaders in narrowing the scope since the types of surveys typically used by school districts represent a smaller subset of broader survey methodologies.

Key Types of Community Surveys

When evaluating survey options, one must first understand the difference between probability and nonprobability samples.

Nonprobability Sampling

As the name suggests, nonprobability survey methodology does not share the feature that everyone in the target population has a chance of being selected, nor can that probability of participation be calculated. Instead, respondents participate because they volunteer or opt in to do so. The most commonly used example of a nonprobability study is a survey offered on the school district's website. Potential respondents must be aware of the survey opportunity, have access to the Internet, and then opt in to complete it. In this instance, the chance of a particular individual visiting the host website and then choosing to take the survey cannot be known. A survey of this type can be augmented by mailing residents a paper survey that can be completed and either mailed to the district office or dropped off. Whether such a mail survey is a nonprobability sample depends on whether everyone in the target population has the chance to receive it and their probability of participating can be calculated.

One of the challenges of a nonprobability survey is that it may be difficult or impossible for the survey's researcher to know if the attitudes of those completing the survey are representative of the attitudes of the full target population. If the people participating in the survey are substantially different from those who do not, results can be biased and inaccurate. Not surprisingly, online nonprobability surveys conducted for school districts typically overrepresent parents and younger voters in significant numbers.

As an example, a suburban school district recently tested support for a school tax election that would raise additional operating money. The district initially completed a random-sample quota phone survey testing its potential tax election proposal. After completing the initial study, the district offered up the same survey on its website to be taken online on a nonprobability, opt-in basis. The chart below compares the results of these two studies across three dimensions: (1) initial support before getting more detailed information; (2) support after receiving information about the proposal; and (3) support at three levels of tax impact.

Because the opt-in survey overrepresented parents and young voters, it should be of no surprise that support measured consistently higher (and likely unrealistic) when compared to the controlled study (figure 5.1).

Given these inherent limitations on nonprobability surveys, the American Association of Public Opinion Research (AAPOR) cautions that, while sta-

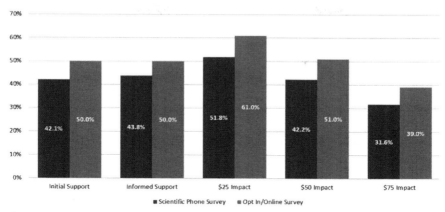

**Comparison of Support from Voters:
Scientific Phone vs. Opt In/Online Survey**

Figure 5.1   Support for School Tax Election (Random-sample Survey Results vs. Opt-In Online Survey Results)

tistical models can be employed to address survey accuracy, it may be misleading to project margin of error for the results of nonprobability surveys.

Probability Sampling

In a probability sample, all individuals in a study's target population have a chance of being selected for the survey sample, and the chance of each person being selected can be mathematically calculated. A well-designed telephone survey using a random digit dialing (RDD) methodology is one example of probability sampling.

An important benefit associated with a random-sample survey of this type is that it yields a margin of error. This means the results from the sample interviewed can be generalized to the target population within the calculated limits. In many studies using this methodology, with a sufficient number of interviews, the margin of error ranges from +/– 4.0 to 6.0 percent at the ninety-fifth confidence level, which provides solid data from which to plan. For this reason, probability-based sampling has been characterized by the AAPOR as the "cornerstone of modern survey research."

It is important to note that differentiating between probability and nonprobability surveys should not lead to the conclusion that opt-in, web-based surveys should not be used. To the contrary, school districts are increasingly using this approach to *supplement* a scientific, random-sample survey. Doing so provides a broader opportunity for residents of the district to have a voice on the issue at hand. In this context, the opt-in, web-based survey can be an effective engagement tool.

When a nonprobability survey is used in this way, school leaders are encouraged to primarily focus on the results of the random-sample, probability survey—given the methodology's ability to calculate margin of error—to guide decisions related to the feasibility of a future tax election. Although there may be statistical methodology to weight the opt-in survey results based on demographics and/or combine results from both surveys, not all survey professionals have this capacity or take this approach, often resulting in less reliable and cost-effective data.

Scientific, Random-Sample Surveys

Assuming the district is convinced that testing feasibility and achieving good alignment is best accomplished with a probability survey and margin of error calculation, the next step is to select the desired methodology among many options in the marketplace. Again, we suggest school leaders focus on two options: *simple* random-sample surveys and *stratified* random-sample surveys. Both meet the probability sampling theory that, if the study chooses respondents randomly and appropriately from the larger population, the survey results will be very close to what one would get by interviewing everyone in the target population (AAPOR).

Simple Random-Sample Survey

The approach, as suggested by its "simple" label, can meet the criteria of a probability sample but does not control for demographic characteristics within the target population. While everyone has an equal chance of being called, some people are more likely than others to actually respond to surveys. This means that, when all phone interviews are complete, the proportion of responses by parent status, age, gender, income, education level, length of time in the community, home location, or other demographic characteristics of interest may be out of sync and not mirror the community characteristics as a whole.

For example, the sample might include too many residents fifty-five or more years in age, too few men, or too many parents. In order to improve the accuracy of the results, there are statistical weighting analytics and protocols that can be accessed, assuming the demographic characteristics of the entire target population are known and are able to be accessed and the survey professional has the expertise to do so.

If a survey professional recommends a simple, random-sample survey methodology, a school leader should inquire about the list he or she is using for the random calls and if it sufficiently covers everyone in the population. It is also important to know if and how results will be weighted and whether the vendor has the demographic information of the target population and research capabilities to do so. It is not uncommon for a vendor to propose a simple, random-sample survey with no mention of its limitations and no intention of weighting the results demographically.

Stratified Random-Sample Survey

A stratified, random-sample survey begins with the premise that, while calls will be random, demographic controls or targets will be established before the phone interviews begin. Successful implementation of this methodology is dependent on the district and survey professional having access to demographic information about the target population so that "counting" can be done in preparation for the data collection.

While desired demographic targets are set before random calls begin, identified subgroups are not capped, meaning that, if the target is hit from a particular group (i.e., women) random calling continues until the overall target for the study is met.

A similar approach, called a random-sample quota survey, also establishes demographic targets before random calling begins, but, unlike a stratified survey, calling stops with subgroups when the target is hit. While this approach can often control better in terms of the sample mirroring the demography of all registered voters, it is not technically a probability survey since some individuals in the sample might not have a chance to be interviewed because random calling is stopped when a quota is hit.

When analyzing demographic "counts" in a sample before doing a phone survey, it is vital to know what proportion of all registered voters have children currently attending the school district. Our experience over time finds that, in most cases, that percentage ranges from 15 to 25 percent, meaning that 75 to 85 percent of a target population of registered voters *are not* current parents. It is critically important when testing support and feasibility of a school tax election that the survey not significantly overrepresent parents, which would likely provide decision makers with a false positive.

Besides parent status, random-sample surveys can control for other demographics, such as age, gender, length of time in the community, likelihood to vote based on past voting behavior over time, race and ethnicity, and location of residence within the district. Similar to early comments, the ability to use this methodology is partly reliant on having a large enough population to stratify into subgroups.

The Basics: Who?

In our view, referendum feasibility surveys should be based on phone interviews with registered voters living within the boundaries of the district. As noted in chapter 2, in recent years we have accessed the registered voter file from L2 and then supplemented the file with other public and commercial demographic and predictive databases. It is from this annotated database that the random-sample calls are made.

In every community, the most active registered voters in the school district will have a very strong influence on the success or failure of any proposal placed on the ballot. Therefore, understanding how these voters react to a proposal is extremely important. When the registered voter database is annotated with other demographic information about voters, the resulting analysis of results provides broader detail in the cross-tabulations. This, in turn, provides a greater depth to the understanding of the results of the school tax election feasibility survey.

Saying a survey will be based on interviews with registered voters does not answer all the questions involved in deciding *who* should be interviewed. There are several ways to design the sample for such a community survey. All have been used to plan successful school tax elections, but each one has distinct strengths and weaknesses.

Some surveys are based on interviews with only the most active voters in the community. Using the definitions developed in the discussion of the voter file in chapter 2, a sample is designed that will cause all interviews

---

IMPORTANT TERMS

The following terms are used in this chapter:

- *Cross-tabulation*—dividing the responses according to the demographic characteristics of the individuals being interviewed; often called "cross-tabs." The simplest is the cross-tab by gender, which allows one to look at the response among male voters separated from the response among female voters.
- *Uninformed benchmark*—a question included in surveys before detailed information is presented to those being interviewed about the need for and cost of a district's proposal.
- *Informed benchmark*—a question included in the survey after information has been presented to those being interviewed.
- *Margin of error*—a measure of the accuracy of the results of the survey.
- *Sample*—the list of individuals who may be asked to complete an interview as part of the survey process. These individuals are selected at random from all the voters in the district.
- *Sample size*—the number of completed interviews used as the basis for a survey.

---

to be completed with very active voters. Because these voters will have a major impact on any election held in the district, this approach will produce the safest recommendations for the district. But this approach may also provide the district with recommendations that raise a minimal amount of money since the most active voters in most districts are older voters without school-age children and are often more conservative.

Another potential limitation with this approach relates to the size of the district since the pool of eligible voters to sample is decreased when you only talk to voters with high voting frequency in past elections.

Some surveys are based on interviews with only voters the database suggests are most likely to participate in an election scheduled for the next date available for a proposal. This approach produces recommendations that are extremely accurate only if the assumptions made about who will probably vote in the next election are not changed by events that occur between the execution of the survey and election day. If events force a change in those assumptions, the survey results may not provide as much insight into the impact of those changes or allow the district to effectively explore the feasibility of placing a proposal on any other available election dates. Similar to what was previously stated, this approach can be used only in large districts because the overall pool is diminished.

The Basics: How Long?

Best practice based on recommendations by AAPOR and many survey professionals suggest that random-sample phone surveys are most effective when the questionnaire is designed to achieve a phone interview time in the 12- to 15-minute range. Depending on the nature and content of the questions, an interview of this length typically translates into a questionnaire of 35 to 40 questions, with no more than two open-ended questions.

The absence of open-ended questions could accommodate a somewhat longer questionnaire and still stay within the recommended time range. Conversely, a questionnaire with more than two open-ended questions would require a shorter questionnaire. Keeping the average length of the interview in the twelve- to fifteen-minute range and letting respondents know at the beginning how long the interview will take meets two important goals of the survey: fewer aborted, incomplete interviews as well as fewer instances of interviewees who rushed their responses in an effort to just get off the phone. Everything else being equal, keeping time on the phone reasonable avoids both pitfalls and should result in better and more reliable data.

The Basics: How Many?

A community survey does not involve calls to all voters in the district. In fact, these surveys are based on interviews with a relatively small number of registered voters. Deciding how many interviews to complete as part of a community survey depends on two factors. The first factor relates to the fact that the primary goal of the survey is to measure overall community opinion with enough precision to predict the feasibility of a school tax election passing. The level of precision or the margin of error in any survey is determined by a formula that is based on the total number of interviews completed for the survey as well as a factor that captures how much the data are weighted. The total number of registered voters in the school district has little or no impact on margin of error. Therefore, we recommend a community survey be based on a minimum of 200 interviews, assuming at least 2,000 registered voters.

Large and diverse districts encompassing unique regional characteristics might require that the sample size be increased to 600 to 800 interviews to accurately reflect regional or demographic differences in the survey results. The majority of our school clients without unique, demographic complexities are well served by surveys with a 300 to 400 sample size. The margin of error for this range in sample sizes typically is in the range of +/– 4.0 to 6.0 percent at the 95 percent confidence level. This level of precision is sufficient to plan a successful school tax election.[2]

The Basics: How?

The interviews completed as a part of this type of survey are done via telephone. The phone has one major advantage over surveys completed through the mail or over the Internet. Before the first interview begins, registered voter history and other demographic information have defined the demography of the district's voting population. The L2 database also includes cell phone numbers resulting in typically 40 to 60 percent of all interviews being conducted on cell phones. As telephone interviews are completed, the stratified methodology uses demographic targets that are carefully monitored, and adjustments are made to the selection of phone numbers from the sample to ensure the population interviewed has the same demographic characteristics as the population of voters in the district.

Mailed surveys can also be an effective way to collect data and a good strategy to engage hard-to-reach respondents if demographic information and a mailing list are available for nearly everyone in the population. If the Internet is the only survey tool utilized in a community survey, one can only hope all demographic groups will respond.

The Basics: When?

The timing of a community survey is a compromise between a desire to collect survey results as close to election day as possible and the need to use those results to plan and shape the district's proposal. In an ideal world, a district would execute a survey a few days before it had to place a school tax proposal on the ballot and have the results back just before the school board votes to call the election. The survey's results would reflect the attitudes of the voters in the district in an economic and political environment that would probably not change significantly before election day.

Unfortunately, completing a survey just before the district must call an election does not allow the district to use the results to shape the proposal, plan the presentation of the proposal to the community, or thoughtfully assess the strengths and weaknesses of the projects to be funded by the school tax election. Therefore, community surveys are generally completed three to six months before the district must act to call an election. Timing the survey in this way affords the district enough time to react to all of the survey's information. Most importantly, the district can ensure whether the projects it wants to fund by asking voters to increase taxes align well with the attitudes and opinions of those local voters.

The dichotomy between wanting to do the survey early so the results can be used and trying to avoid too much time between data collection and voting has increasingly resulted in districts doing two surveys. This approach allows an initial survey to be completed ten to twelve months before the district must act. These early surveys are used to explore the possible ways in which tax funds will be spent so projects can be developed in alignment with community opinion.

An early survey will also identify projects that are out of alignment and require extensive community discussion if voters are to understand why and how these projects are important to the district's health and strength. Early surveys are also useful in districts in which recent events make it clear that local voters may have a less-than-positive opinion of the district's ability to plan or spend tax dollars wisely. By exploring voter opinion twelve to fourteen months before the likely date of a tax election, an engagement and communications plan can be developed addressing concerns among local voters about the district's fiscal skills and overall performance.

If an early survey is completed, a second tracking (shorter) survey is generally planned just a few weeks before the district must make a final decision about the content and tax impact of a proposal on the ballot. This survey will retest tax tolerance and assess the impact of any communication with local voters resulting from the first survey.

The Questionnaire

The community survey's questionnaire needs to test the impact of information about the district's school tax proposal and the level of community support. Typical questionnaires will also weave in some open-ended questions for qualitative purposes and message testing. In designing the questionnaire, it is important to understand that school tax elections are different from all other elections because the only thing that can motivate an individual to vote to give away money is information about *why* the district needs the money. Other elections—even other referendums—don't have the kind of direct, immediate impact on household budgets that one finds in a school tax election.

In a candidate race, many voters will make up their minds as soon as they find out the candidate is a Republican or a Democrat. In a school tax election, the only party that exists is the uninformed party—voters who will vote "no" because they do not know anything (or enough) about the proposal.

To understand clearly what information persuades voters to cast a "yes" vote, a community survey must test the impact of presenting voters with more and more information about the tax proposal. The first step in the interview is to ask everyone if they favor or oppose the district's proposal before any detailed information is presented. For a bond election, the question might read as follows: "The Brisbane Elementary School District may place a bond measure on the ballot that would increase property taxes to raise the funds needed to renovate the district's schools and classrooms. Would you favor or oppose such a proposal?"

When the survey is designed to explore a tax increase to raise operating funds, the question might read: "The Stillwater Area Public Schools may ask local voters to approve an increase in local property taxes to provide the district with the funds needed to avoid budget cuts, the elimination of teaching positions, and an increase in class size. Would you favor or oppose such a proposal?"

These types of initial questions are referred to as the *uninformed benchmark* (figure 5.2). In this context, uninformed means that interviewees are responding initially to very limited information. As the examples illustrate, the statements provide very few details about the proposal. The interviewee knows it involves an increase in local taxes. But the question

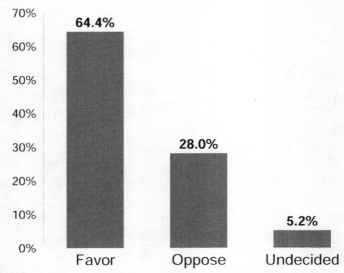

Figure 5.2   Support Based on Uninformed Benchmark

does not present any information about the cost of the proposal to the individual being interviewed nor does it elaborate on the way the requested
funds will be used.

The purpose is to identify those voters who will support virtually any
reasonable proposal the district places on the ballot. Identifying this population tells the district the size and demographic characteristics of its base
of support.

Once the uninformed benchmark question has been asked, details about
the district's proposal are presented. These questions attempt to break the
whole proposal down into its smallest parts and test each part separately.
Therefore, instead of following the uninformed benchmark with a four-
or five-sentence statement describing the need for the school finance
proposal, each idea that might be included in such a short statement is
presented in a separate question to test how voters react.

In the following example, instead of stating that funds will be used to
restore both the music program and the physical education program, two
questions are presented. The first reads: "Funds will be used to restore
reductions made in the music program." The second seeks a reaction to
the idea that "funds will be used to restore reductions made in the physi-

cal education program." Probes in this section of the survey are typically randomized in terms of order heard by the respondent.

For a construction or renovation proposal, separate questions would be used to explore voter reaction to the use of funds, for example, to replace plumbing, upgrade electrical systems, install new energy-efficient heating systems, or build new classrooms and buildings. The district will be able to clearly see which parts of the proposal cause voters to become more likely to support it and which do not. Responses to questions presenting information about the school tax proposal are ranked according to the number of people made more likely to support the proposal by the information presented (see figure 5.3).

Once all the statements about the proposal have been presented, everyone is asked again if they would favor or oppose the proposed measure. This question is called the *informed benchmark*. The responses to this question allow a district to see if information has increased support for the proposal (see figure 5.4).

Pct More Likely	Statement
72.7%	10. Leaks in the aging water system are common. One recently resulted in the flooding of a school library.
67.9%	16. Funds will be used to replace the forty year old gas lines at the local schools.
65.8%	9A. Funds will be used to replace the forty year old water lines at the local schools.
65.5%	12. Funds will be used to create an energy management system that will make the heating and cooling of all district buildings more energy efficient.
65.3%	14. Funds will be used to provide expanded libraries and media centers at all schools.
60.0%	15. An independent oversight committee will ensure funds are spent responsibly and according to the district's board approved plan.
59.2%	11. Funds will be used to improve student safety at drop-off areas and in parking lots.
57.4%	8. Funds will be used to replace existing 40 year old single pane classroom windows with more energy efficient windows.
56.0%	13. Funds will be used to replace portable classrooms with permanent classrooms.

Figure 5.3

Chapter 5

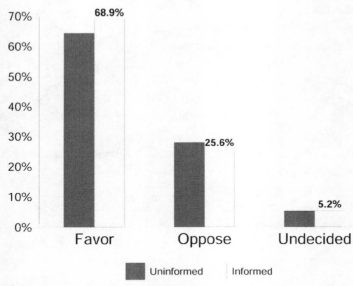

Figure 5.4 The Informed Benchmark

If support increases at this point in the survey, the individual items presented need to be ranked to see which items had the greatest impact. The statements that made the largest number of people more likely to vote for the proposal will form the core of the presentation of the district's school tax proposal to the community. If, on the other hand, support does not increase—or worse, goes down—the individual items described in the survey will need to be carefully evaluated to determine the reason. By doing this, the district can better align its needs to the community's appetite for additional school projects.

Analyzing the overall results of the uninformed and informed benchmark questions is only the first step in the process of understanding the data collected in a community survey. The cross-tabulation of this data by the demographic characteristics of the voters interviewed greatly expands our understanding of the responses. By cross-tabulating survey results, the district learns if men and women are equally supportive of the proposal or if older voters show the same level of support as younger voters.

The demographic characteristics of the voters come from two sources. Some are collected as the interviewees answer specific survey questions. For example, each person interviewed is asked if he or she has school-age children in the household. If they do, the individual can then be asked if the children in the household go to public or private school.

WORDSMITHING WITH SPLIT-SAMPLE QUESTIONS

In addition to exploring voter reaction to the projects and programs that might be funded by a tax increase, split-sample questions explore voter reaction to the words chosen to describe those projects and programs. Interviewees are divided into two equal groups. Half of them are presented with one version of a question. The other half are presented with a version of the same question in which key words or phrases have been changed. For example, a survey was done for a district that wanted to use bond funds to create what its administrators called "high school parent/student centers." When asked, people at the district level could explain that these were areas proposed for use as tutoring centers. They called them parent/student centers because they expected parents to be among the volunteers coming to the centers to help tutor students. The name "parent/student center" had become so attached to this project that district leaders had started writing it into communications material intended for the entire community. We decided that we needed to test the impact of using this language before proceeding further with such communications materials. To do so, half of those interviewed were asked if knowing that "funds will be used to create parent/student centers at local high schools" made them more or less likely to support the district's bond proposal. The other half were presented with a question that read, "Funds will be used to create areas at the high schools where parents and other volunteers can tutor students." The results made it clear that referring to "parent/student centers" did not convey enough meaning to the voters in the community. Less than half (or 49 percent) were made more likely to vote for the bond by this information. An explanation that these were tutoring centers made 60 percent more likely to vote "yes." As it continued to present information to the community, the district was able to avoid the use of its own jargon and more clearly explain the purpose of this expenditure.

Based on everyone's response to these questions, the responses to the benchmark questions can be divided according to "parent status" (figure 5.5). This is the *asked demography* developed in the survey, part of the new normal as it relates to the decreased need to include demographic probes in the questionnaire since L2 and other commercial data sources come with this information. One caveat, however, is to evaluate and/or test the accuracy of demographic information accessed from such databases. Self-reported demographic information obtained through the questionnaire can often be more accurate.

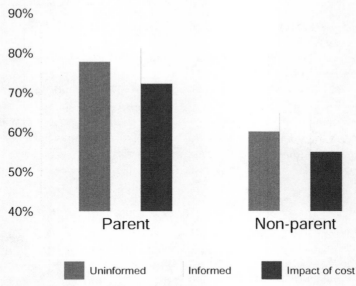

Figure 5.5   Parent Cross-Tabulation

The voter file also contains demography available for cross-tabulation. This information is *file demography*. It can include information about the interviewee's voting activity, their voter registration date, where they live, whether the voter is a renter or homeowner, and other demographic variability in the voter file database. The cross-tabulations completed from file demography are generally the most important to the successful planning and execution of a school tax election.

One approach to postsurvey cross-tabulations processing is a process we call Insights and Implications, based on a model developed by Chris Deets of Strategic Communications. While this approach might appear somewhat complex at first blush, it is ultimately simple and highly critical to successful planning. Like a seasoned journalist, Insights and Implications probes for the "story behind the story"—processing the valuable data from the survey results, sorting through it to identify significant differences compared by demography, and then identifying implications that may arise from acting (or, in some cases, not acting) upon the results.

The first step of data mining using the Insights and Implications approach involves looking for large discrepancies and gaps in the percentages. These gaps serve as signals to your team that "something is there, so we need to look closer and try to understand." More often than not, these gaps represent information that may be counter to prevailing assumptions; the larger the gap and the more counterintuitive it is, the greater the need for analysis. As the data are mined and the gaps are identified, they are placed into the "Insights" column in order of the size of the gap from largest to smallest. Divining insights from data is the first step in converting data into actionable information.

The second step is developing implications from the insights. This ensures the wisdom from our insights is translated into actions to help lay the foundation for successful planning, whether that is a referendum or a new strategic plan. Developing implications starts by asking two questions of each insight. The first question is, "If we take action and ensure these percentages remain the same or even grow, would that help achieve the planning objective?"

The second question flows naturally from the first, "If we take action and try to alter these percentages, would that help achieve our goals?" Usually there are a number of insights gleaned from any set of data. However, focusing on a limited number that show the greatest discrepancy—and thus hold the greatest promise for action—is the best use of the team's resources.

The third step in the Insights and Implications model is to develop goals and an action plan to address the top priority areas uncovered by the survey results. These goals should be concrete and attainable and

---

INSIGHTS AND IMPLICATIONS

Figure 5.6 illustrates how the differences found in the cross-tabulation of survey results can be used to plan specific actions by the district and the citizens' campaign that will be formed to support the district's proposal. In the second example, the impact of budget cuts is presented to voters in terms of class size increases and in terms of the loss of teaching positions. Overall, there is very little difference in the way voters reacted to these statements. When told that budget cuts had increased class sizes, 47 percent said the information made them more likely to support the district's proposal. When told that eight teaching positions had been lost, 51 percent said they were more likely to vote "yes." The gender cross-tab allows us to see, however, that these responses are not equally effective. Describing the impact of recent budget cuts in terms of class size increases does not have the same impact on men as it does on women. The same is not true of a description of the number of teaching positions lost. The Insights table helps the district effectively use the information in the cross-tabs by forcing it to write down the implication of the results and define an appropriate action.

We Asked ────→ **We Learned** ────→ **That Means** ───→ **So We Will**

INQUIRY	INSIGHT			IMPLICATION	ACTION
Bond funds will be used to install advanced instructional technology at each of the district's high schools to including the tools that have become a part of a 21st century education.				The instructional tools that are a part of a 21st education do not resonate as well with non-parents as they do with parents and alumni parents.	Target the way in which we use information about improvements to the technology— prominently to parents and alumni parents and not emphasized as much to non-parents.

	K-12 PARENT	ALUMNI PARENT	NON-PARENT
MORE LIKELY	67.6%	65.1%	55.9%
LESS LIKELY	10.8%	13.4%	19.5%
NO DIFFERENCE	21.6%	21.5%	24.5%

Budget cuts have increased class sizes for students in grades 4 through 8.			Men and women have very different reactions when told that class size has been increased in grades 4 through 8.	See below.

	MALE	FEMALE
MORE LIKELY	37.5%	54.5%
LESS LIKELY	23.9%	17.9%
NO DIFFERENCE	38.6%	27.7%

Budget cuts have eliminated 8 teaching positions			Men and woman have a very similar reaction when the impact of budget cuts is expressed in terms of the number of teaching jobs impacted.	Express the impact of budget cuts in terms of the loss of teaching positions versus increases in class size to minimize the disparity in reactions between males and females.

	MALE	FEMALE
MORE LIKELY	50.0%	52.0%
LESS LIKELY	20.6%	18.4%
NO DIFFERENCE	29.4%	29.6%

I would never vote for a tax increase no matter what the money would be used for.			Resistance to any new tax increases with age.	The campaign will not ignore older voters but will focus more energy on voters under 55 years of age.

	18 TO 34	35 TO 54	55 AND OVER
AGREE	16%	24%	31%
DISAGREE	84%	75%	68%

Budget cuts will reduce the amount of time reading and math specialists can spend with students struggling with these basic skills.			Reducing the time specialists can spend with students struggling with basic skills has its greatest impact on the district's most active voters.	The loss of reading and math specialists will be communicated prominently to very active voters. It will become a secondary message for less active voters.

	VERY ACTIVE VOTER	ACTIVE VOTER	LESS ACTIVE AND NEW VOTER
MORE LIKELY	63.8%	54.3%	48.4%
LESS LIKELY	33.6%	43.5%	50.0%
NO DIFFERENCE	2.6%	2.2%	1.6%

Figure 5.6

include standards for evaluation and specific expectations in terms of the time to complete them. Insights and Implications provides an effective way to translate data into actionable goals while maximizing the value and positive impact of a scientific, random-sample survey. The Insights and Implications model, shown in figure 5.6, illustrates the conclusions derived from a thorough review of detailed survey results by demography and, more important, the actions that will be taken as communications and campaign activities are planned prior to a school tax election.

Exploring Reactions to Cost

Up to this point, the survey has explored the impact of information on the level of support available for a potential school tax referendum. The next step is to explore the impact of cost information on the base of support created by this information. The questions that complete this task are the *tax tolerance questions* that need to be included in each survey. In terms of testing the general tax climate, one approach would include a probe seeking a response to the following statement: "I would never vote for a tax increase, no matter what the amount or what the money raised would be used for."

Respondents are asked to quantify their agreement or lack thereof along a five-point Likert scale. Based on hundreds of scientific surveys over decades, we have found that, in the vast majority of communities, 15 to 25 percent of respondents agree with the "no tax" statement. Responses in this range reflect a normal tax climate, and one that could be receptive to a well-designed ballot proposal. In a recent suburban survey, however, an eye-popping 60 percent of respondents agreed with the no-tax sentiment. A survey response of this kind immediately suggests the need for the district to slow down, thoughtfully diagnose what might be causing this outlier, and take the time to repair the tax election climate before bringing a ballot proposal forward.

In addition to testing the overall tax climate within a community, a scientific survey should also evaluate tax tolerance on a proposal-specific basis. The key to producing an accurate result, however, is to understand that voters will react best to a cost that specifically relates to how much money the proposal will remove from their household budgets. Therefore, to determine if local voters will support a $30 million school bond, one does not ask voters whether they would prefer a $20 million, $25 million, $30 million, or $40 million bond. Numbers like these are too large for voters to relate to their day-to-day expenses. After all, no one being interviewed will be asked to pay the entire cost of the bond. Nor can they be expected to have any detailed knowledge of how much it might cost to lower class size, build a new school, or renovate their neighborhood's middle school.

Therefore, a survey should present numbers that describe the average annual cost of a $30 million bond to the average homeowner or the cost in terms of the average assessed value of a home in the community and ask voters to react to these numbers. The survey's results will provide the district with an optimal annual cost to the average district homeowner. The district's financial advisers will use this number to calculate the amount of money the district can raise for building construction or renovation.[3] The same applies to proposals that will raise operating or technology funds.

ONE TEST IS NOT ENOUGH

Assessing tax tolerance usually requires that two types of questions be included in a survey. The first type presents a very specific cost to those being interviewed after they have heard information about the need for a tax increase. Such specific cost questions generally read as follows: "I want to add one additional fact. If you knew that the proposed school bond would have an average annual cost of $30 per $100,000 of assessed value, would you favor or oppose this proposal?" At another place in the questionnaire, voters are also asked to react to three to five other possible costs for the school finance proposal. The responses to these questions develop a trend line that allows the district to see how support decreases as cost increases. This trend line can be used to project an acceptable tax rate if the response to the presentation of a specific cost fails to achieve sufficient support.

Looking for Agreement

Exploring voter reaction to more complicated statements often requires the use of a more sophisticated analysis tool. One of these tools is the use of classification trees to quickly identify the demographic groups most likely to agree or disagree with a statement about the public schools. This analytical tool allows us to better identify groups, discover relationships between groups, and predict future events. In such an analysis, classification software is asked to evaluate one question by exploring the response among the demographic groups available in the survey.

In the example, a district asked us to explore voter reaction to the statement, "Since the state has not provided adequate funds, we need to step up and help." A very large number of the voters in the district, 72 percent, agreed or strongly agreed with this statement. By applying classification tree analysis to this response, we were able to show the district that the positive response to this statement varied by gender and the geographic location of the voter within the district. Figure 5.7 presents the tree generated for this

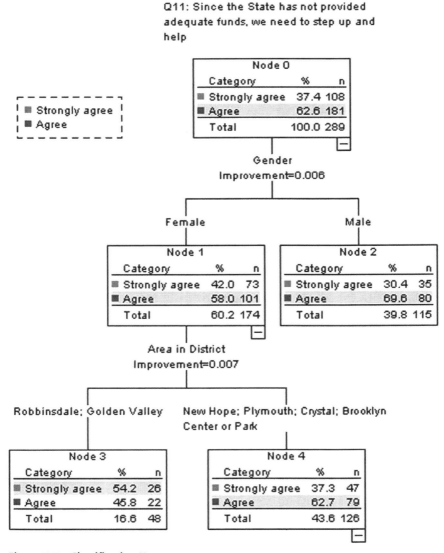

Figure 5.7   Classification Tree

question by SPSS for Windows. The first branch is defined by the gender of the voter being interviewed. Women are more likely to strongly agree with this statement than are men. The second branch relates to areas within the district. Women in the Robbinsdale and Golden Valley areas of this district are the most likely to strongly agree with this statement.

Applying this technique to several statements about public education, the campaign was able to craft highly targeted, highly effective messages as it worked to build support for a school finance proposal.

How Are We Doing?

At this point, the survey has collected enough information to know whether a school tax election is feasible, to identify the projects that best align with community opinion, and to determine an acceptable cost for the proposal. Good design of a survey questionnaire also provides the opportunity to test the impact of messages with different demographic groups and to evaluate how the district is perceived qualitatively. These questions could range from overall satisfaction with the quality of education to managing finances or keeping the public informed. These questions develop a district profile that adds depth to the knowledge gained by testing satisfaction and climate within the district.

This added dimension is extremely important in the planning of a successful school tax election. As noted in chapter 1, if too many voters have a negative opinion of the district's performance—especially its fiscal capability—it will be extremely difficult to win community approval for any proposal (Lifto & Morris, 2000). These questions also allow the district to see how many voters feel they cannot evaluate the district. If this population is large, the district knows both it and the citizens' campaign in support of its proposal will need to introduce the district to voters *and* ask for money. This type of information is much more useful while *planning* a school tax election than finding it out in the *middle* of a campaign launched to support a school tax proposal.

During the development of the questionnaire, school districts can also explore opportunities to benchmark current perceptions with either earlier surveys and/or national surveys on common probes. Comparing current perceptions to prior surveys is possible when a school district is collecting survey data on some schedule over time (e.g., every three years).

In that case, the questionnaire can incorporate identical questions that have been used in past surveys and ask them again if still relevant. Qualitative probes measuring satisfaction lend themselves to this approach. A related strategy that can be considered is to benchmark against probes that have been used in national surveys in order to compare and contrast with local results.

As an example, we have obtained permission from Langer Research Associates, the survey research partner with the Phi Delta Kappa annual poll on public education, to use questions from its national survey in local surveys done with school district clients. This apples-to-apples comparison puts local results in context and provides relevant and interesting planning data for the district (figure 5.8).

Figure 5.8

How about a Focus Group

Focus groups are sometimes used in the early stages of planning a community survey and can provide some insight into specific questions that might be worth asking. In some cases, focus groups could include different demographic groups, some of which might present a challenge to the approval of a local school tax increase.

Focus group participants are usually presented with the best argument the district believes it can make for its proposal. The focus group participants are encouraged to question, discuss, and interact with each other concerning the content of the district's presentation. As they are doing so, focus group participants are observed, and careful notes are made concerning the items in the presentation to which they react very positively or very negatively. A focus group produces more subjective information than does the community survey.

Used together, they can enable a district to develop a strong, persuasive message for use during the campaign communications effort. Likewise, post survey, some districts will pull together focus groups to react to the survey results, potentially providing school leaders with a deeper understanding of the raw data.

Notes

1. Portions of this chapter originally appeared in "Insights and Implications: Mining Data from Scientific, Random-Sample Surveys," Don E. Lifto, PhD, & Chris Deets, published in *American School Board Journal*, National School Boards Association, January 2015.

2. The American Research Group provides a handy margin-of-error calculator at http://americanresearchgroup.com/moe.html.

3. In most cases, tax tolerance should be evaluated in terms of the cost per year. Doing so usually aligns the costs being presented in the survey with the costs that will be presented in the legal documents that must appear on the ballot with a local school tax proposal. Testing the impact of a rate on a monthly basis will produce a more positive result. After many years of working with the results of annual versus monthly tests, we are convinced the more positive monthly results reflect the inability of the average voter to multiply by 12. Measuring tax tolerance in this manner does not preclude the campaign committee from translating its message to a monthly cost for its communications.

Chapter 6

Ballot Structure[1]

Crafting an effective ballot question traditionally encompasses three dimensions: content, cost, and structure. In light of the ballot question's central role in election day success, aligning it with a community's values *and* willingness to pay becomes a key policy decision for the school board. Although states vary in terms of how much ballot structure and language flexibility is extended to school districts, school leaders must use available data to determine the community's tax–cost threshold prior to shaping the ballot question.

All districts should explore the degree to which the laws of their state will allow the ballot question to include descriptive language that will help voters understand how these tax dollars will be used. Scientific survey results and the resulting voter file target structure position school leaders to respond to the content, cost, and structure dimensions, providing the school district and proponents with a sound foundation from which to campaign.

Content

Simply put, the content is the "what" of the district's proposal. Is it a new middle school? A new high school? Reduced class sizes? Expanded Advanced Placement courses? Expanding a STEM program to STEAM? Regardless, the research is clear—districts that scientifically test voters' preferences and design ballot questions reflecting the community's values are more likely to prevail on election day. As described in chapter 5, a well-designed scientific survey is a prerequisite to achieving alignment in terms of both the "big" question (e.g., will it be a new high school or middle school?) and specific elements of the proposal.

Safety improvements may be a top priority in one community, whereas voters in another school district may identify remodeling needs or reducing class sizes as most important. Scientific surveys can test multiple options to see which investments will result in increased support by those registered voters most likely to cast ballots. Demographic and predictive databases, discussed in chapter 2, also provide enhanced opportunities to identify which demographic groups (and the size and voting patterns of each) support key components of the potential ballot initiative.

Cost

Whether it is a major investment in new construction or in lower primary class sizes, putting the right "what" on the ballot is only half the battle. When asked in postelection surveys why an election failed in a community, "cost was too high" or "taxes would have gone up too much" are two of the most frequently cited explanations by voters. Therefore, determining the community's appetite for spending is the second key dimension to consider when crafting the ballot question.

As Salvatore Sclafani pointed out in his 1985 study of New York budget elections, "The Determinants of School Budget Election Outcomes in New York State: A Forecasting Model," each district has its own collective appetite for educational services. The outcome of an election is largely a function of whether the community's collective demand is in harmony with what the school district offers in the form of a ballot proposal.

To achieve this alignment, school districts are increasingly using pre-election surveys to test the tax climate and determine the proposal-specific maximum tax increase voters are most likely to approve. A well-designed survey can explore the voters' collective "comfort zone" and help align the district's proposal with what residents most value and are willing to pay for via a tax increase.

In addition to measuring the general tax climate, effective surveys also test voters' reactions to a range of tax increases related to a potential ballot proposal. Unless there is a finite, fixed cost for a specific project, we typically recommend testing tax tolerance at either three or four price points with equal intervals between each tax increase. We also randomize the order in which respondents hear the range of proposed tax increases to avoid having interviewees sense they are being taken up or down the ladder, potentially affecting their responses.

As the line measuring support intersects with the fiftieth percentile (or a higher threshold in states requiring a supermajority for passage), the survey clearly reveals at what tax impact the district will likely fail to achieve a "yes" majority. With that in mind, wise districts back off from this maximum acceptable tax rate far enough not only to factor in the survey instrument's margin of error but also to provide for an additional margin for victory.

Avoiding pushing the envelope on tax impact, in relationship to tax tolerance as measured by a survey, becomes more vital the longer it is between the collection of survey data and election day. Making any untested assumptions about tax tolerance is risky, but assuming tax tolerance will be significantly better in four, six, or eight months as compared to today may condemn a proposal to failure when it's placed on the ballot.

Structure

What's the best way to structure a bond or operating election ballot? First and foremost, experience would strongly suggest that, if the district can achieve its objective in one ballot question—at an acceptable tax rate—it will be much easier to communicate what is being proposed, why it is needed, and the cost to taxpayers. Running a school tax election with two or more ballot proposals can become exponentially more difficult to explain to your community.

When one ballot proposal falls short for any number of reasons, it can pay to take a lesson from history—military history—using the strategy of "divide and conquer." This military strategy summons the image of a legion of Roman chariots careening wedge-like though a line of foot soldiers or a cavalry dividing a unit of soldiers from its ammunition and supplies. Children regularly heed this battlefield lesson when they strategically pit one parent against the other to get what they want—and school officials looking for success at the ballot box can heed it as well.

In the context of school tax elections seeking additional funding, divide and conquer can become a political strategy in the form of a split ballot. By splitting a proposal, it's sometimes possible to divide the "no" vote, lessening the likelihood and intensity of organized opposition. By taking this approach, a school district has the potential to get more out of two questions than it could realistically expect in a single proposal, and it improves the odds that at least the first question on the ballot will be successful.

Splitting the ballot can also be an effective strategy in cases in which the tax tolerance is low, when the community has a history of organized opposition, or when survey results suggest voters are demanding more choice. Although still unusual, some school districts are responding to this unbundling strategy in a big way—particularly after one or more losses— by serving voters a smorgasbord of three or more ballot questions that are either contingent or freestanding.

State law will dictate in some cases whether subsequent ballot questions can be contingent on the first one passing or that each must stand alone for an up or down vote. In some cases, splitting the ballot can serve to lessen the likelihood and intensity of opposition by providing smaller bites and greater choice.

Whether you're running a property tax election in California, a technology election in Missouri, or a major bond proposal in New York, your school district shares one thing in common with all others—a stratified electorate ranging from boosters to detractors. In between those two groups is often the largest block: the persuadable voters, most of whom can be described as either "soft yes" or "soft no." In addition, some voters have no opinion at all as the election campaign begins and are best described as undecided.

Behavior at the extreme ends of the voter spectrum is both predictable and uniform. Boosters will consistently vote in favor of a school proposal, and detractors will vote overwhelmingly against it. Splitting the ballot into more than one proposal might have a minimal (but positive) effect on your most ardent boosters and detractors, but it can significantly alter voting patterns among the persuadable voters, moving some from what would have been a "no" vote on a single-question ballot to a "yes/yes" or "yes/no" vote on a split ballot proposal.

As the chart shows (figure 6.1), a two-part ballot can split the "no" vote and leverage additional "yes" votes in support of the main question. Two or more questions might also have the psychological effect of lowering

Single Question Q1 $20 million	Proposal	Split Ballot Q1 $14 million Q2 $6 million
100% "Yes" votes	Boosters	100% "Yes" Votes
70% "Yes" votes	Soft "Yes"	80% "Yes" Q1 60% "Yes" Q2
50% "Yes" Votes	Undecided	60% "Yes" Q1 40% "Yes" Q2
30% "Yes" Votes	Soft "No"	40% "Yes" Q1 20% "Yes" Q2
100% "No" Votes	Opponents	100% "No" Votes
50% "Yes" 50% "No" Toss-Up	Outcome	Q1 56% "Yes 44% "No" Q2 44% "Yes" 56% "No"

Figure 6.1   Use of Ballot Splitting to Alter Voting Patterns

the stakes in terms of perceived tax consequences and make it less likely organized opposition will form.

Organized opposition is the foe of special elections requiring taxpayer approval. Paraphrasing from the work of Philip Piele and John Hall, the grandfathers of school tax election research, school issues are uniquely susceptible to group-based attacks. Therefore, the more organized the opposition, the more likely the election will fall to defeat.

Splitting the ballot can bring two new, powerful factors that will influence the presence or absence of organized opposition as well as the intensity of these groups. First, splitting the proposal makes it more likely the school board can keep the cost of the main question within the community's appetite for spending as determined by the pre-election polling. Second, and consistent with Marketing 101, the individual price tags of two or more separate ballot questions will always seem less than the total cost of a single question carrying the full weight of the proposal. Staying within the community's collective comfort zone and lowering the "sticker shock" by using two ballot questions can ease concern about the election, discourage formation of organized opposition, and reduce the energy of a proposal's detractors.

How and when should a district consider splitting a ballot question? We suggest school districts keep a few simple criteria in mind as they decide whether to lump all funding needs into a single question or split a proposal into multiple questions. Splitting the ballot should be considered if one or more of the following factors exist:

- The cost of a single-ballot question exceeds the comfort level of the public in terms of a tax increase as measured by a pre-election survey.
- The district has a history or likelihood of organized opposition.
- The district's proposal can logically be divided between what is absolutely essential and what is important but of secondary priority.
- A block of citizens solidly supports the second proposal and is willing to work for the first one because passage of their favored second proposal depends on it (assuming that a contingent ballot question is allowed under state law).

Jumping on the split-ballot bandwagon is not the right strategy in all situations and will not guarantee victory. Sometimes, splitting a proposal is simply not feasible. For example, a district cannot propose to fund half of the new middle school in Question #1 and the other half in Question #2. In other situations, the strategy of splitting the ballot may result in confusion or unwanted controversy. School districts vary greatly, and every election is conducted within a unique and complex context.

The "splitting" strategy should be considered when a district is expecting a close or highly contested election or when the cost of the whole package exceeds the community's comfort level. A carefully designed split ballot, aligned with a community's priorities and willingness to pay, could be the difference between winning and losing a school tax election.

Splitting is not the only structural characteristic of the ballot question to consider. In some instances, districts might offer three or more questions on a single ballot or, if allowed by state law, design a contingent relationship between two or more proposals. Districts must also deliberate the order of the ballot questions when two or more proposals are presented.

Although we do not cite specific research on this point, successful practice strongly suggests school districts should always lead with their top priority. Common sense would dictate that most voters will associate multiple ballot questions with an increasing and cumulative impact on their taxes as they move down the ballot. Ballot fatigue—resulting in fewer "yes" votes for subsequent proposals as compared with the first question—must be considered. Everything else being equal, it is more likely the first proposal will pass than a second or third question.

In states that allow contingent questions, a second or third ballot proposal can be designed to be contingent on the first question passing. The actual ballot language for a contingent question might begin by stating, "If Question #1 is approved by the electorate, do you also want to authorize. . ." Under what set of circumstances might it make sense to structure a contingent ballot question? One example is in rapidly growing school districts in which construction bonds are needed to build additional school buildings.

If the district cannot afford to absorb the increased operating expenses of a new school and enrollment growth does not generate enough new revenue, a district might request more operating money in Question #1 and then have Question #2 provide bonding authority to build the school. The intent of this ballot structure is to communicate to the voters that the district cannot afford to build a new building without the additional revenue to staff and run the school.

The same strategy can be used for an operating levy with Question #1, for example, seeking additional revenue to add more teachers to reduce class sizes, with a contingent Question #2 requesting more resources for gifted and talented or remedial programs. In this example, the split ballot structure with a contingent second question accomplishes two goals.

First, the structure of the ballot clearly differentiates between the district's core mission and most urgent need and other important, but secondary, proposals. In essence, the district is telling the community, through the structure of the ballot questions, that if it cannot afford to put a sufficient number of teachers in the classroom, then it certainly is not going to invest in other programs.

The second advantage of this ballot structure is that it allows for an exercise in community-based decision making that can help blunt the attack of those in opposition. By proposing a two-part ballot and asking for direct community involvement in setting the school district's priorities, it is much more difficult for opponents to haggle over minor details in any part of the proposal.

The best campaign in the world will not be successful if the content, cost, and structure of the ballot questions miss the mark. School districts must use information from the scientific survey and voter file to align their proposal with their community. A carefully developed ballot question provides advocates with what all salespeople seek—the right product at the right cost in the right package.

Note

1. Portions of this chapter originally appeared in "Lessons from the Bond Battlefield," which appeared in the November 2001 *American School Board Journal*. Copyright 2001 National School Boards Association.

Chapter 7

Ongoing and Strategic District Communication

"Plan the work and then work the plan," goes the saying. This sentiment is as true for communication during an election campaign as it is for any other aspect of the process. Developing a referendum communications plan—one that begins long before the school board votes to hold an election—is a critical part of a winning strategy.

While this chapter will focus on how to develop and implement the district's information campaign, two points should be made:

- Effective communication with staff, parents, and community members does not start when an election is on the horizon. Effective communication should be part and parcel of how school districts operate on a daily basis. Keeping your community informed and engaged will not only help when a referendum comes along, but it can help school districts attract and retain quality staff, support student achievement, maintain and increase enrollment, and build trust in the school district, among other things. Ideally school districts will have a school public relations officer on staff to plan and manage this work. Just as school districts employ trained human resources personnel to manage the staff hiring, training, and retention processes, so too should school districts have trained school public relations staff to ensure their communications efforts are planful, strategic, and effective.[1]
- While other chapters outline the specific roles and responsibilities of the citizens' "Vote Yes" campaign, having a solid communications plan applies to their work as well as to the district's. In fact, the citizens' committee communications plan should align with the school district's plan to ensure messages, tactics, and timing support and to reinforce each other.

WHAT IS SCHOOL PUBLIC RELATIONS?

According to Don Bagin and Donald Gallagher, two well-respected former leaders from the National School Public Relations Association (NSPRA), school public relations is "systematic, continuous, two-way, honest communication between the school district and its publics."

And in the words of Glen Broom, a nationally respected public relations professional, author, and professor, "Public relations is an essential management function that identifies, establishes, and maintains mutually beneficial relationships between an organization and the publics on whom success or failure depends."

Four-Step Communications Planning Process

Strategic communicators use a four-step process to develop their communications plans: Research, Planning, Implementation, Evaluation (R-PIE). Also known as RACE (Research, Analysis, Communication, Evaluation), this process helps ensure that communication is based on research, focused on goals, targeted to key audiences, strategic, and planful.[2] Without a communications plan, school districts tend to simply implement a string of tactics. This scattershot approach may hit a target or two, but it usually will miss many key marks and often end in failure.

STEP 1

Research

The first step in preparing your referendum communications plan is research. What do you know? What do you need to know?

- What is the district's referendum history? Looking back ten to twenty years, how many times has the district asked voters for their support through a referendum? What is the success rate? What was voter turnout like in different election environments? What percentage of parents voted?
- What is your community's context? Have you had contentious issues that have drawn parents and nonparents alike to school board meet-

ings to voice their displeasure? Have you engaged with your community in good times as well as bad to ensure their voices are heard and responded to? Have you been cutting budgets, or are you a growing district with a lot of new families moving in? Do you have active civic and senior organizations that support your school district and can help serve as ambassadors for a referendum request?

- Did you conduct a community survey (see chapter 5)? What does the survey tell you about messaging, tax tolerance, and communications sources? Are there differences in how men respond versus women, senior citizens versus parents, likely voters versus less likely voters?
- What else will be on the ballot? Are there other requests for taxpayer support? Are any of the races likely to be contentious? Will this be a high- or low-turnout election?
- What does the community know about your needs—whether they are financial or facilities related? Has your community been involved in assessing your needs, through a facilities task force, strategic planning, or budget assessment process?
- What kinds of communications tools do you use? Do you have an established connection with your senior citizens? Do you send out regular mailings about the school district? What communications systems do you have in place to connect with your staff and your parents? Do you have any established feedback loops, such as an "ask us" email address, school board listening sessions, town hall meetings, or Facebook Live events?
- What are the early and absentee voting rules and locations for this election? When does early voting start?

The answers to all these questions are key pieces of information upon which to base your plan. For example, if you recently lost a referendum and are returning to voters with a revised proposal, a key message in your materials will likely be some form of "We listened, and we responded by changing our request."

If you know that senior citizens respond more favorably to your need to update your buildings by replacing roofs and old heating systems, but your parents respond more favorably to your plan to add classroom space and reduce class sizes, then your messages should be tailored to each audience accordingly.

If this will be a noisy, contentious election with high voter turnout, you will need to do your best to reach as many voters as possible, multiple times and multiple ways. If, on the other hand, it is an off-year election with very little on the ballot, then your focus will be on ensuring parents are clear about the consequences of success and failure for their children's educational experience, that they realize the importance of their vote, and (if appropriate) early voting information is easily understood and accessible. For those school districts that take the time to determine what percentage of their parents voted in past elections, the news can often be quite sobering. Some school districts will use a message of low parent turnout as a motivator. For example, one district repeatedly told parents (both through the district materials and the "Vote Yes" materials) that only 25 percent of parents voted in the last election—and if they wanted the classroom additions and lower class sizes that would be funded through a successful referendum, it was absolutely critical that each and every parent vote this time.

Research can be as simple as reading a report or having a conversation— or it can be as elaborate as conducting a survey or engaging a community. Either way, it is fundamental to a successful school communications program.

—Bill Banach, APR, Past President of the
National School Public Relations Association

STEP 2
Planning

Once you have done your research, you can start to develop your plan. The best plans are literally written down, both for a visual road map and checklist, so everyone can be clear on what you are doing, when, and why.

The *first part* of your written plan is a list of the key findings from your research. You will refer back to these findings often—both as you are planning and while you are implementing your communications strategies. They should guide what your goals are, who your target audiences are, what your key messages are, and what tactics will be most effective.

The *second part* of your plan is a list of your goals. While the primary goal is to win the election, there are subgoals you need to achieve in order to get there. For example, if your research showed that past parent turnout was low, a goal will be to increase parent voter turnout. Other common goals are

- to provide clear, accurate, and timely information about the referendum to all residents, with a focus on target audiences;
- to ensure all employees, parents, and other key stakeholders understand the referendum, know where to get more information, and are encouraged to exercise their right to vote; and
- to support clear and consistent message delivery through a number of communications channels.

These goals, which are based on your research, will help you later identify what specific strategies and tactics to use.

The *third part* of your plan is to define your target audiences. A common response is that "all voters" are your target audience. While this may be true to some extent, it's not very helpful. Targeting your communications efforts and messages to particular subgroups is much more effective and, frankly, more realistic, given district resources. Target audiences can be groups such as current parents, prospective parents (e.g., preschool parents), staff, retired resident staff, recent graduates, high school seniors, elected officials and other opinion leaders, and school volunteers.

As school districts serve increasingly diverse populations of families, the way they need to communicate must mirror that diversity. "English only" publications are a thing of the past in most communities. Knowing which languages you should translate materials into also involves knowing that some cultures do not use the written language as much as the spoken. For these communities, training your cultural liaisons in the facts of your referendum so they can share them directly will be a critical part of reaching these parents.

As described in chapter 10, the citizens' campaign will have its own set of target audiences, usually defined by likelihood to vote and projected level of support for the referendum.

The *fourth part* of your plan is the key messages. These messages are based on your research and should answer four questions:

- What is being proposed?
- How much will it cost me?
- Why should I vote for it?
- What happens if it passes or fails?

In most states, school districts are limited to providing only factual information, leaving advocacy to the citizens' committees. The core messages for both campaigns should be the same, but the citizens' committee should add emotion and compelling reasons to vote "yes" to their versions of the messages. Key messages may be statements such as the following:

- If approved, these funds would help us maintain our schools, improve athletic spaces, and invest in classroom technology to support student learning. (To reinforce this key message, this school district used "Maintain, improve, and invest" as its referendum tagline and included it in the district's referendum logo.)
- Voters have not approved a property tax increase to fund school needs for nearly fifteen years.
- This levy increase would enable us to invest more in our students and our schools while limiting additional budget cuts.
- Strong public schools are directly linked to the well-being of our city and strong property values.
- We are one of the only school districts in our area without a voter-approved operating levy to support classroom needs. (In this community, research showed residents valued being seen as better than their neighbors.)
- After the voters rejected our last referendum, we spent nearly a year listening. The school board's unanimous decision to bring these requests to voters was based on extensive research and community input on how best to meet students' needs and maintain district facilities. (This district was returning to voters a year after losing a facilities request.)

As much as possible, tie your messages to students and their education. While your research will help define what matters to your voters, stressing the impact on kids and communities is usually more meaningful to a community than the dollars or the bricks and mortar.

CORE AND SUBORDINATE MESSAGES

The core message is the one thing you want to be sure voters remember when they cast their ballots. Following is an example of core and subordinate messages for a bond referendum:

- Core message: A new middle school is important to our students, staff, and the future of this community. Our students deserve to be educated in a school that is safe, up to date, and spacious enough to meet the needs of our growing student body.
- Subordinate message (targeted to older voters): eighty years ago, our parents and grandparents built a school for us. The old school has served us well, but this is an opportunity to reinvest and give back, making sure that our children and grandchildren can reach their full potential in a safe and modern school.
- Subordinate message (targeted to preschool parents): Your child is growing and changing every day. Middle school is another time in a child's life when a lot of changes happen. This proposal includes building an up-to-date middle school that is safe and can address the important needs of middle schoolers, just as our preschool programs address the needs of our youngest learners.

In support of your key messages, you will have complementary subordinate messages tailored to specific audiences. These subordinate messages will focus on aspects of your request that matter to that particular group.

In addition, you may have secondary messages that address other information you learned from your research or that is tied to your goals. For example, in a district that learned the community was wary of its financial management skills, the referendum materials also included these secondary messages supporting fiscal responsibility:

- Our school district has received the Certificate of Excellence in Financial Reporting for sixteen consecutive years, considered the gold standard in financial reporting from the Association of School Business Officials International. We also have streamlined our operations to generate $650,000 per year in utilities cost reductions, saving taxpayer dollars.

MESSAGE SANDWICH

The message sandwich strategy, developed by Jeff Ansell, president of Jeff Ansell and Associates, not only helps to articulate and refine core and subordinate messages but also provides a handy tool for individuals caught in the glare of the television camera. Like a well-constructed sandwich, there are top and bottom slices to hold things together and lots of good stuff in between to provide substance, flavor, and texture.

The Top Slice

The top priority of this school district is constructing a new middle school. The current building is more than eighty years old and unsafe and can no longer meet the needs of our students and programs. New construction makes more sense and avoids excessive tax money wasted on repairs.

Between the Slices

- The current building has serious structural, safety, and classroom deficiencies.
- It is more cost effective over time to construct a new school rather than pouring more money into repairing the old building.
- We are losing dozens of families and tens of thousands of dollars every year to neighboring schools with better middle school facilities.
- The new school will offer a modern library, up-to-date science and computer labs, and adequate space for a growing student body.
- The new school will provide students and staff with a safe environment absent concerns about asbestos, mold, and poor ventilation.

The Bottom Slice

A new middle school is a good investment and vitally important to our students, our staff, and the future of this community. Our students deserve to be educated in a school that is safe, up to date, and spacious enough to meet the needs of the growing student body.

Implementation

Once you have gone through the first two steps of research and planning, you are ready to decide what tactics and tools to use. Many districts start their planning process here, which is a common—and often fatal—mistake. Your tactics and tools need to be aligned with your research and goals, focused on your target audiences, and consistent with your key messages.

Tactics are the things you will do and activities you will undertake. Tools are the materials you will produce to use as you implement your tactics. Both should be selected based on their ability to reach your audiences and help you achieve your goals.

Common tools used in district communications plans include e-newsletters, websites, printed fact sheets, social media graphics, video, sample ballot with callouts explaining the legal jargon, district mailings, automated calls from principals to parents, and PowerPoint presentations. Depending on your capacity, audiences, and goals, you may add additional tools, such as podcasts, texts, postcards from teachers to parents, Facebook Live events, online forums, stickers, banners, Google AdWords, Facebook ads, lawn signs, leaf bags, door hangers, and other ways to share your message or that of your campaign.

Two partial examples to illustrate how these pieces align and support each other are:

Example #1

Goal: Provide clear, accurate, and timely information about the referendum to all residents, with a focus on target audiences.

Target Audience: Current parents, prospective parents (e.g., preschool parents), staff, and retired resident staff.

Figure 7.1   Sample Referendum Logos

Tactics:

- Create a referendum logo and theme for use on all materials.
- Create a referendum website that includes basic facts on the main page, a resource toolkit, FAQs, voting information, tax impact, and ways to "learn more" (referendum email, phone line, public information sessions).
- Provide board members with a key message handout.
- Using key messages, produce a referendum fact sheet and Quick Facts bookmark.
- Review referendum information at all-staff school kickoff.
- Train school teams on referendum facts and help them develop school-specific communication plans for sharing the district's referendum materials.
- Include referendum overview in district newsletter mailed to all residents.
- Prepare letter from superintendent to all retired staff who live in the district, giving them a referendum overview and inviting them to a special coffee where they can learn more.
- Schedule a series of "Did you know?" facts about the referendum for social media—include referendum logo and link to referendum website.
- Provide schools with short referendum articles to include in their school newsletters for the three months leading up to the election.
- Meet with all employee union groups to review the referendum and answer all questions.
- Attend each school's staff meeting twice prior to the election to review referendum and answer all questions.
- Develop a simple fact card targeted to preschool parents and provide copies to all school district early childhood classes and programs.
- Send a letter with a referendum poster and preschool fact cards to all childcare providers in the school district with an offer to host a referendum coffee session at any childcare facility that would like to schedule one.
- Produce a two- to three-minute video about the referendum, featuring kids and teachers.

- Use the video content to create four thirty-second videos for social media use.
- Include referendum articles in every issue of a weekly e-newsletter sent by the district to all parents.
- Translate referendum fact sheet into Spanish and Russian.
- Meet with cultural liaisons to develop culturally specific outreach plans.
- Host and promote two public information sessions at different ends of the school district.

Example #2

Goal: Increase turnout among parents (preschool and K–12).

Target audiences: Current and prospective parents.

Tactics:

- Contact cities and county to determine exact early/absentee voting rules and locations.
- Develop a simple and engaging "Voting Early Is Easy!" fact sheet with easy-to-follow steps and locations for early voting (include referendum key messages on the back of the fact sheet).
- Include early voting information on Facebook the day it begins and reinforce the option every other week until election.
- Create a petting zoo at the early childhood center during early voting hours, hand out a referendum Quick Facts bookmark, and encourage parents to stop next door at the voting center to vote early.
- Provide area childcare centers with referendum Quick Facts bookmarks and "Voting Early Is Easy!" fact sheet.
- Ask principals to reinforce the message that parent turnout was only 25 percent in the last election whenever they are talking with parents about the referendum.

Tactics Grid

A helpful way to map out your tactics is to create a spreadsheet or grid to serve as your planning guide.

Table 7.1

Tactics	Timing	Audiences	Led by	Done?	Budget
Include board's decision on referendum in staff e-newsletter	July 20	Staff	Communications	X	$0
Develop referendum logo and theme	Aug. 1	All	Communications	X	$500
Write series of "Did you know?" tidbits about referendum for social media channels	Aug. 20 (Sept. 1–Nov. 5)	Parents, Staff	Communications		$0
Produce animated video explaining the referendum in an engaging and visual way	Aug.	All	Communications		$3,000
Create referendum fact sheet, website, Quick Facts bookmark, and PowerPoint	Aug.	All	Communications		$500
Share referendum video at back-to-school staff kickoff and invite staff to submit questions to referendum email	Aug. 30	Staff	Superintendent		$0
Meet with teacher leaders in each building to answer referendum questions	Sept.–Oct.	Staff	Superintendent		$0
Train school teams on referendum and communications plans	Sept. 10, 6–8 pm	Parents, Staff	Superintendent, communications		$250
Promote and hold public information sessions	Oct. 1 & 10, 6 pm	All	Superintendent, communications		$0
Include referendum facts in every issue of parent e-newsletter from district	Sept. 1, Oct. 1, Nov. 1	Parents	Communications		$0

As mentioned earlier, school districts that have well-established communication systems in place prior to an election have a significant head start when a referendum comes along. Your key stakeholders are used to hearing from you, and they likely have high levels of trust in what you say. You have communications tools in place that you can use to amplify and share your referendum messages.

One example of a communications strategy that can be in place prior to a referendum is targeted outreach to senior citizens. Our schools belong to our communities, making it incumbent upon us to communicate with our community members on a regular basis. As noted in chapter 1, our communities are aging, making senior citizens an increasingly larger share of our voting population. This reality makes reaching seniors increasingly important, both for a source of school volunteers and because seniors regularly vote. A school district in Minnesota has a newsletter that is sent to senior citizens quarterly, informing them of upcoming events open to the public and sharing student and school successes. During a referendum, this newsletter can include information about the ballot request and is likely seen as a trusted source. Some school districts create special senior passes that allow senior citizens to attend school plays, sports, and other events at no or low cost. These efforts not only show your senior citizens that you value them but also helps keep them connected to your schools— a connection that can pay off come election time.

THE IMPORTANCE OF BUILDING TRUST THROUGH ONGOING COMMUNICATION

According to Edelman's Trust Barometer:

- When a company is *distrusted*, 51 percent will believe *negative* information after hearing it one or two times, whereas only 15 percent will believe positive information after hearing it one or two times; and
- When a company is *trusted*, 51 percent will believe *positive* information after hearing it one or two times, whereas only 25 percent will believe negative information after hearing it one or two times.

Social Media

A word about social media. As social media evolve, platforms come and go—and who uses which platforms for what purposes also changes. While social media have a place in both the district and "Vote Yes" campaigns, they are merely one tactic of many. Some campaigns will spend a lot of time and energy on social media, to the detriment of more targeted and effective tactics. Other campaigns will use social media to push out only their own information but won't monitor what is being said by others, so they lose the opportunity to respond when appropriate.

Social media are also free, easy ways for opponents to spread falsehoods and attack the district. Depending on the forum and the context, it may be better for a parent to respond to the opponent rather than the district on social media. Monitoring the channels, knowing how widely they are followed, and being strategic about who should respond are important features of today's election environment.

One example is a neighborhood-based platform called NextDoor, which is like a cross between Facebook and Craig's List. Since this is primarily a platform used by residents to share with those who live in close proximity, any referendum news or criticisms are best handled by the residents themselves. For a "Vote Yes" committee, that means monitoring the content via residents who live throughout the school district and responding so the district doesn't have to.

Knowing your audience is critical in the use of social media. Who is actively engaged on each of the social media platforms you are considering? Will they engage with information about your referendum on a particular platform, or will they see it as an intrusion in what they view as a "social" space? Can you develop messages and visuals that support your case while also being engaging and shareable?

For districts that have established a strong social media presence in advance of their campaign, this can be a very effective and targeted tactic. If you do not have much of a social media presence, you can certainly try to build it during your campaign—but consider it a secondary tactic, and work on building your following after the campaign is over so it's ready for the next time.

Dealing with Opposition

Whether you have one detractor or face an organized "Vote No" campaign, effective communication can help. The ultimate goal is to remain focused on your own messages and plan. How and where you respond will depend on your community, who your detractors are, and what concerns are being raised.

In general, you should respond to any concern honestly, openly, and in good faith—but do not remain visibly engaged with a detractor beyond a question or two. For those who want to continue beyond a round or two of questions, one strategy is to invite them out for coffee or to the district office to meet and discuss their questions face-to-face. This approach stops some detractors in their tracks, while others will take advantage of the time to ask many more questions.

Some detractors will never be on your side no matter what you say. Others want to distract you and the community from your messages and focus on unrelated issues or falsehoods. Some can become vocal supporters if treated properly. Some superintendents make it a point to meet with anyone who has concerns to show that they are accessible and willing to talk. When they say, "all politics is local," how to respond to detractors certainly bears this out.

The Four Cs:
Clear, Concise, Consistent, and Compelling

Much of the communication produced by school districts and campaign committees is notoriously lacking in clarity, conciseness, consistency, and compelling language. In postelection surveys across a variety of school districts, citizens routinely blame poor communication as one of the key reasons finance elections failed in their community. Their collective fingers of blame, which are pointed at school boards and superintendents, cite jargon, legal language, and "educationese" as barriers to both understanding and supporting a school district's proposal.

To be fair, many states require specific and often obtuse language in ballot questions, making it more difficult to communicate clearly in the language actually placed on the ballot. There is no excuse, however, for district or campaign materials that fail to communicate effectively.

Message Box

If you anticipate or encounter significant opposition during a school tax campaign, the "Message Box," as described by Paul Tully and Diane Feldman in Politics the Wellstone Way (Wellstone Action, 2005), provides a template to create and focus your message before producing specific media in support of the campaign. Figure 7.6 depicts the four key questions necessary to fleshing out the Message Box. Figure 7.7 uses the same planning framework to flesh out campaign messages related to a facility referendum. Both the message sandwich described earlier in this chapter and the message box emphasize a vital strategy in campaign communications—development of core and targeted messages comes before design of print and electronic media. While this would appear on the surface to be a no-brainer, it is a common mistake for campaigns (and school districts) to start writing and designing communications either without a plan or irrespective of the plan.

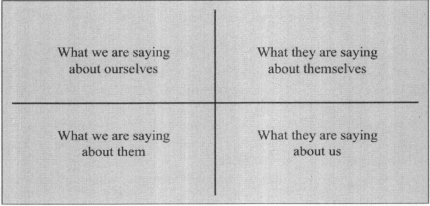

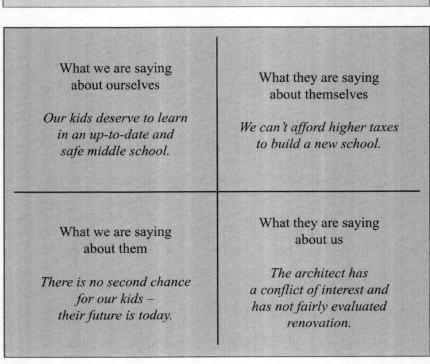

Figure 7.2

THE 80/20 RULE

The 80/20 rule dictates "staying on message" while employing a stealthy block and parry technique with your toughest critics. To avoid your public meeting morphing into two hours of complaining about maintenance problems at the high school, use the 80/20 rule to get back on message. When questions or critics take the focus off message:

- Respectfully acknowledge;
- Briefly respond; and
- Return to your message.

At the end of the meeting, the goal should be that at least 80 percent of the talk time was focused on your message.

Question at Public Meeting

"You guys keep talking about building a new middle school instead of what really needs to be done. The high school is a maintenance mess and a hazard to students. I say build a new high school, instead, along with some remodeling at the middle school. The high school is my main priority, and that's where the money should go. We don't need a new middle school."

Responding Using the 80/20 Rule

"Thanks for your comment. You bring up a good point. The facility task force, made up of citizens just like you, has identified eight priority maintenance projects at the high school, all of which need to be done and all of which will be done if this bond election passes. The most pressing need, however, is a new middle school. The old building turned 80 this month, is too small for a growing student body, does not meet state fire and safety codes, and does not support the needs of students who wish to achieve a first-rate education. A new middle school is our first priority, and the old school must be replaced. We can build a new middle school and improve the high school with one-third less cost to our taxpayers."

The following are some (albeit negative) cases in point of what *not to say* during your next school tax election. All of the following were taken from school district or campaign materials:

- "Expand student access to educational continuity throughout the system and enhance learning opportunities through concentration of age groups and the associated benefits of teaming methodologies."
- "Accommodate modern education program theory, including information-age management, outcome-based education, and global education."
- "Expansion will include technology curriculum integration into the technology/multimedia education area."
- "New Knowledge Center will provide library, computer stations, and exploratory learning opportunities."
- "We do not have a multipurpose/academic/performing arts/community meeting area for school and community use."
- "The legislature severely limited the use of operating levies in the late 1980s. The attempt was to promote equity in funding across the state, but the result was a freezing of differences among districts."

Arne Carlson, who served as Minnesota's governor in the early 1990s, often chided politicians and bureaucrats who used confusing language. In so doing, he challenged them to pass the "barbershop test," which implies that, if your average Joe or Jane at the barbershop can't understand what you are talking about, the broader public can't either. Too much of what schools produce during school tax elections fails this test, thus confusing or alienating the very people who could be persuaded to vote "yes" on election day.

In addition to clarity, school leaders also need to be concise in producing materials in support of a tax election. It's important to strike the optimal balance between providing enough information without overloading voters with volumes of text they will not read. Districts should provide information in different formats for those who will spend only thirty seconds listening, for those who will read something for three minutes, and for those who will spend thirty minutes or three hours learning everything they possibly can about your referendum.

Consistency is critical. Your key messages should be delivered many times and in many ways to your audiences. In real estate, the mantra is "location, location, location." In communication, it's "repeat, repeat, repeat."

We counsel school district leaders that, when they are getting tired of saying their referendum messages, their audiences are maybe—*maybe*—just starting to hear them. People are bombarded daily with messages from so many sources—email, social media, television, newspapers, mail, neighbors, friends—that it's no wonder not much can actually stick. So, even though you may have explained your key messages in countless presentations, included them in dozens of emails, shared them via all your social media platforms, and written about them in mailings, always act like it's the first time. For your audiences, it may be (or at least they may think it is!).

The last of the 4Cs—compelling—exhorts school district and campaign communicators to use the richness of their language, graphics, photographs, and video to generate some passion and imagery that will persuade voters to remember the campaign's core messages and support the proposal. Given the limitations of what school districts can do relative to advocating for the proposal, addressing the "compelling" standard is mostly left in the hands and imaginations of campaign committee members. Drawing insight from the community survey and their own experiences, seasoned communication experts can effectively affect voters' attitudes with compelling messages and designs. One example of a compelling theme is that of a turtle (figure 7.3). The turtle, which symbolized

Figure 7.3

a core message that this suburban district was "dead last" in terms of class size, was a powerful centerpiece of this successful campaign.

Evaluation

The last step in a well-designed communications plan is to evaluate. Win or lose, it is important to debrief staff, key volunteers, and other community members.

How did people react to information from the district's or the campaign's materials, both of which were intended to present essential information about the district's proposal? How well did the core message from the campaign committee complement the informational material from the school district? Did feedback from public meetings, emails, and other forums demonstrate the public understood the content and rationale for the district's proposal? Did your tactics help you reach your goals? Did voter turnout match your projections—and which areas of the district supported the proposal? What worked, what didn't, and what should you consider for next time?

This information can be obtained in a variety of ways, including debriefing sessions, in-depth interviews, focus groups, surveys, and feedback from other communication professionals in a jury of peers. Answering these questions represents the first step toward building a foundation for success in your next facility or operating referendum. Take notes, and store them along with samples of all communication materials—district's and citizens' campaign—to review when the next school election comes long.

If you expect to run a school tax election in the future, the time to start building your public relations program is now. Often, less than 30 percent of registered voter households contain children enrolled in the local public schools—certainly not enough voters to win most school tax campaigns. This demographic reality makes it all the more important for school district and campaign leaders to execute the four steps—research, plan, implement, evaluate—within the context of a broader public engagement plan.

Public relations that is grounded in engagement with the public, focused on clear goals, and ongoing throughout the year will provide a solid foundation and substantially improve your chances on election day.

Notes

1. For those interested in learning more about the value of an ongoing school district communications program, visit the National School Public Relations Association website at https://www.nspra.org/getting_started.

2. This four-step process is a cornerstone of public relations and is standard practice for professionals who have received their Accreditation in Public Relations (APR). To learn more about this PR planning process, visit http://www.praccreditation.org/apply/apr/, and review the "Four Step Process" chapter in the "APR Study Guide" listed under "Resources" on that site.

Chapter 8

Planning Framework

If you skipped to this chapter to review our suggested campaign plan, turn back to the beginning of the book and start reading. Every part of this book is designed to help you plan and execute a successful campaign in your school district. It does not, however, contain a copy of "The Patented Winning Campaign Plan." The reason is simple. No single plan can meet the needs of *every* school district and *every* election environment.

But there is a framework and process that will allow you to create one for your district. In the context of campaign planning, most of the strategies summarized in this chapter focus on the purpose and structure of the advocacy group working in support of the district's tax proposal. This does not diminish, however, the critical importance of *connecting and coordinating* the informational role of the district with the advocacy work of the campaign committee.

The process of designing and writing a campaign plan will be one of the most challenging tasks a school leader will ever undertake. Preparing for, planning, and executing a campaign will, if done properly, distract the superintendent, the school board, key staff, and the parents from the tasks they perform during a normal school year. This is true even when the district or campaign is able to access external consulting help. Depending on the size of the district, there often is a need to plan internally on how the necessary work of the district will get done and think through the roles of key leaders.

The scope and content of successfully planning and executing a campaign has a great deal in common with the tasks surrounding the preparation of Thanksgiving dinner. If you routinely plan and cook Thanksgiving dinner so that everything arrives on the table hot, handsomely presented, and cooked to perfection while the guests take their seats just as the last of the serving dishes are placed on the table, you have an understanding of the skills it takes to plan and execute a school tax referendum.

And, just as you spent time learning the techniques of preparing this annual family feast from parents and relatives, you need to take time now to learn an approach to campaign planning that will give you the necessary tools to create a winning campaign plan.

Basic Rules

Before beginning a discussion of our approach to planning, however, there are some basic rules that apply to all school tax campaigns. These rules will apply throughout the planning process. Although following all of them will not guarantee you a victory, ignoring them will ensure a loss.

- *Start planning early.* If you are reading this book in January and know your district will place a proposal on the November ballot, do not put the book down and figure you will start applying what you have learned closer to election day. Given all that must be done to fully prepare a school district for a school tax campaign, January is awfully close—maybe too close—to November. In most cases, give yourself at least twelve months. And remember that vacation schedules make the summer a very difficult time to get anything done. Never assume you will get half of what you planned to do on the campaign done between June and September.
- *Make sure the campaign plan coordinates the activities of the school district and the citizens' campaign.* The laws of each state place various restrictions on district activities. But throughout the planning process, you are creating a unified campaign in which the district and citizens will have clearly defined, coordinated roles.
- *Review all district policies that may affect execution of the campaign.* These policies may include data privacy policies, access to parents' phone or email contacts, use of school buildings and grounds for advocacy groups, use of staff emails, or use of the district's autodialer system for reminders to vote.
- *Find and use outside talent where it will expand the expertise found in your district office and school buildings.* A school tax election will require the school district to use skills and talents that are not a part of its regular operations. While no district's budget is unlimited, experience has taught us that a school tax election is not the time or place to be

BUILDING YOUR TEAM

- Make sure you have the legal and financial help you need. Even though the district has lawyers and financial planners who help with day-to-day operations, the district will need to consult lawyers and financial advisers who specialize in school tax proposals. Lawyers who specialize in school tax proposals will provide you with the legal deadlines with which you must comply and an outline of the legal documents that must be prepared before you can go onto the ballot. Financial advisers can provide you with accurate estimates of how much the proposal will cost the average voter in the district.

- Consult with outside architects and engineers. In many districts, the facilities department is quite capable of describing and documenting the challenges facing the district's classrooms and buildings. It is important to have this work checked and rechecked, however, by outside architects and engineers familiar with the questions voters will ask the district once a proposal is placed on the ballot.

- Realize curriculum review is an ongoing process. Preparation for a campaign may require the district to bring in outside facilitators to expand the normal review process to include an attempt to quantify and make specific the district's vision of the classroom education it wants to provide in the future.

- Hire communications and community research specialists. Although the district may have excellent communications and assessment departments, there are communications and community research specialists who work almost exclusively with school tax proposals. Do not hesitate to learn from them how survey research and communications planning differ when the goal is a "yes" vote on a local proposal.

- Seek out campaign consultants who can assist in the process of turning your desire to address a financial challenge or improve your schools into a concrete plan for winning on election day. Such a consultant should never replace the army of school people you will need to win, but his or her understanding of how to structure a campaign can save you the time you might otherwise spend "reinventing the wheel."

- If a campaign plan is not written down, it does not exist.

penny wise and pound foolish. A wise district starts early in assembling the team that will help it plan and execute a victory at the ballot box.

Now, let's look at a framework for examining your district's situation and creating a campaign plan that will meet your specific needs. If your district has never been on the ballot, this process will help you think through all the steps involved in creating an effective, winning plan for your first campaign. If you have campaigned before and lost, it should help you look at your district, its needs, and your community in a different way. In *Reframing Organizations*, Bolman and Deal (1991) introduce four "lenses" or "frames" for organizational analysis:

- Structural
- Human Resource
- Political
- Symbolic

Viewing your situation through these lenses and approaching the next election with this framework in mind can help you engage in the process of winning with an integrated, comprehensive plan.

The Structural Frame

The structural frame relates to coordinating, organizing, controlling, planning, goal setting, and clarifying expectations. From this frame, strategies develop. If this is your district's first referendum effort, use all the data available in an annotated voter file and in demographic district maps to understand *who* the voters in your district are. There will be key questions to answer. Are district parents registered to vote? If they are registered, do they participate—or does it take a presidential election to get most of them to the polls?

Does the ethnic background of your student and parent population match that of the population of registered voters? Very often, district leadership is surprised to find that, although more than half of their students are from minority populations, minorities still make up a small percentage of the voting population in the district. If your district has been on the ballot sometime during the past few years, expand your knowledge of the voters in the district by completing a postelection analysis. Learn everything possible about your district through the statistics that define it and its voting population.

Expand what you have learned by using survey research where appropriate to explore the degree to which the community around you understands the challenges facing the district and shares your goals for the future. These research tools will allow you to develop a clear understanding of the community's core values. You can then work to present the community with a school tax proposal that is well aligned with their expectations.

Fully evaluate all district communications by asking someone from outside the district to review the materials you have been producing. Work with your state's public relations association or a private consultant to understand which parts of your current communications program are working and, most important, which are not. During this process, it is very important to find those places in your communications where you are using educational jargon. Though such language is extremely useful as you communicate with colleagues and peers, it may not communicate your challenges, goals, and solutions effectively to the broader community.

Finally, as you learn more about your district, use this material to write a detailed and comprehensive plan. Capture details about the challenges you face. If you cannot quantify the ways in which additional tax funds will be spent, add to your timeline the steps needed to complete a facilities audit or curriculum review. After an evaluation of district communications, outline the steps that will be required to improve the program's effectiveness.

Following the creation of an annotated voter file and, possibly, postelection analysis, determine whether parents within the district are registered and whether they vote. If they are not regular voters, make sure the plan includes ways to increase parental registration and participation. If there are areas of the district that may oppose—or always have opposed—school taxes, make sure the plan captures your best thoughts and ideas about how you will overcome these potential "no" votes. When the plan is finished, move on to recruit capable people to execute it.

The Human Resource Frame

The human resource frame relates to involving people through an under-standing of each individual's feelings, needs, preferences, abilities, and desire for participation. Begin with an honest evaluation of the leadership being provided by the school board, superintendent, administrators, teach-ers, staff, and parent volunteers.

Evaluate that leadership as it applies to the events of the current school year and then investigate the district's past. Base the evaluation of the leadership available in the district on qualitative and quantitative data. A realistic audit of the leadership resources available in your district will have a direct impact on the success of the campaign and the district's abil-ity to meet the needs of students through the ballot proposal.

In the broadest sense, effectively engaging citizens in the campaign and deploying their talents wisely is reflected in the pyramid structure below. The goal of the Engagement Pyramid—in the context of the human re-source frame—is akin to stretching a rubber band horizontally at the base while simultaneously stretching it from bottom to top (figure 8.1).

At the base of the Engagement Pyramid, the mission is to broaden the number of community members (parents and others) who are knowledge-able about and involved in the campaign. The other dimension of the Engagement Pyramid is vertical, moving ideal task performers from low levels of engagement to increasingly higher involvement and responsibili-ties at the top of the triangle.

Matching the campaign's needs to the volunteers you recruit can es-sentially be thought of as loading the campaign from a human resources point of view. For those of you who are movie buffs—young and not so young—an analogy from the cinema would highlight the movies *The Dirty Dozen, The Magnificent Seven*, and *Ocean's Eleven*. What these box-office hits had in common was that each plot had a *very* difficult challenge to overcome, and all three used the same strategy to overcome overwhelming odds—they recruited the perfect team (ideal task perform-ers) to get the job done. Likewise, recruiting the perfect campaign team for your next tax election is a critical step in winning on election day.

Just as there are professionals who can help you review district com-munications, there are professionals who specialize in helping school districts plan and execute school tax campaigns. Do not hesitate to bring

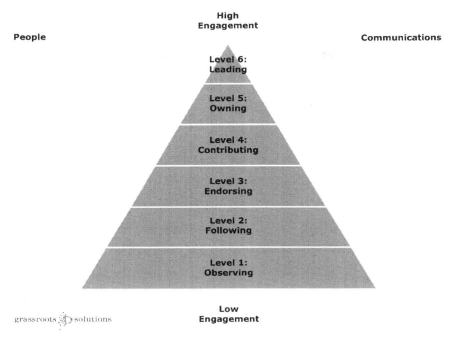

People

High
Engagement

Communications

Level 6:
Leading

Level 5:
Owning

Level 4:
Contributing

Level 3:
Endorsing

Level 2:
Following

Level 1:
Observing

Low
Engagement

grassroots solutions

Figure 8.1   Engagement Pyramid

these consultants into the district to assist in the evaluation of your leadership resources. Because they have gone through the process of planning and executing school tax campaigns more times than any superintendent ever should, they can offer valuable insight into the human resources available in your district. They also can provide invaluable support as you work to motivate your election team and win your campaign.

Finally, as you work to identify and solicit leadership for your campaign, use the *ideal task performer* philosophy. No matter what job there is to be done, there is an ideal task performer to do it. Think for a moment about two jobs that almost every campaign has: someone who coordinates the activities of the campaign volunteers and someone who actively recruits those volunteers. If two people have expressed an interest in these jobs, the campaign will most likely be best served if the detail-oriented introvert takes on the role of coordinator while the extroverted chair of the PTA takes on the job of recruiting people to work in the campaign. The more critical the task, the more important it is to find ideal task performers.

As you read, pay special attention to the verbs that were just used. Leadership will be *identified*, *solicited*, and *recruited*. This process involves work and time, all of which must be accounted for in your campaign plan. Many campaigns end the night the superintendent or school board president calls a meeting in the gym to ask if anyone would like to chair the district's upcoming school tax campaign.

The approach we are recommending strongly suggests that developing a leadership team is both strategic and "hands on" and discards the notion that the superintendent would call a meeting in the school cafeteria to find volunteers to chair the campaign. Identifying, soliciting, and recruiting the leadership needed for a campaign is a process. Provide time for it in your campaign plan and define the specific steps you will need to take to complete it. Finally, remember that all leaders—whether staff, parent volunteers, or community members—must also be chosen with a keen sense of how they will be perceived by the public.

In addition to leaders, every campaign needs volunteers. The best campaigns apply Tom Sawyer's philosophy and involve a lot of people. If five volunteers might complete the job of canvassing a neighborhood near the district office, recruit ten. For every job where it makes sense, involve as many people as possible. Their involvement will make light work of many of the campaign's most difficult or mundane tasks. In addition, the more that teachers, staff, and parents invest in the campaign—both through the hours they volunteer and the dollars they donate—the more likely they are to remember to end the campaign by casting a ballot. As you develop a campaign plan, quantify your need for volunteer hours and list the ways in which volunteers will be recruited.

DIFFICULT AND MUNDANE?

Not all tasks that must be completed to win a campaign are exciting. A sign used to hang in the government relations office of one of the nation's largest teacher organizations. It read: "Campaigns take the brightest, most energetic people in your organization and ask them to complete the most boring, mundane tasks they can imagine."

The Political Frame

The political frame focuses on the conflict, negotiations, influence, and interplay among different constituencies, interest groups, and organizations. This frame will include how you approach the leaders of the political parties in your community and how you plan to contact those groups of voters that your postelection analysis, geovisual demographic mapping, or community survey tells you are most likely to resist your effort to raise taxes.

Begin with the positive by identifying community VIPs and soliciting their opinions and support. Seek out "blockbuster" endorsements, especially from individuals who "everyone" might assume will oppose your school tax proposal. If you have been on the ballot and lost, this will include looking for converts who will change from a public "no" to a public "yes."

Often, as a school leader, you are not able to directly influence the members of the community most likely to oppose you. But that does not mean that you cannot reach out and ask for the help of supporters who can influence those groups or individuals. For example, a district that lost two school tax elections knew that its proposal failed due to an antitax vote in the community. No argument the school community made concerning the need for classroom programs and well-maintained buildings influenced the leaders of these antitax voters.

Before its next election, the district solicited and received the support of members of the business community. With their help, they built a strong case for the school tax around the idea that local property values were being threatened by a weakened school district. This argument, presented with the help of the local business community, was able to influence some of the antitax voters, thus reducing the number of "no" votes cast to the point that the district passed its proposal.

A second example involved some background research. A school district lost a major school tax election because of the outspoken opposition of the local taxpayers' association. After the loss, district leadership brought in the help it needed to assess the funding sources that were supporting the taxpayers' groups. Once identified, the district was able to talk with supporters who worked for many of the companies that were supplying the taxpayers with campaign funds. Those employees were able to slow down, and in some cases stop, the flow of funding to the taxpayers after they talked to their bosses and coworkers about what the loss meant to classroom programs throughout the district. As you develop a campaign plan, think about ways that you can convert or isolate potential opponents. Quantify the steps involved and provide ample time in your campaign calendar.

The political framework also demands that you be very clear about how a loss affects the community and its children. All school tax campaigns live with some built-in limitations. You cannot build your campaign on the threat that a loss will mean that you will shut down the entire third grade. School leaders, principals, and teachers will do everything in their power to keep schools and classrooms open, regardless of how much funding the legislature or the community takes away. But, as it approaches a campaign, district leadership must be willing to state very clearly the logical consequences of winning or losing on election day.

Thinking through those consequences and writing them down is an essential part of planning. You must identify what is at risk and be willing to tell people that their vote will make a difference. You cannot exaggerate because school will be open on the day after the election and the community will see what happens. People will not vote "yes," however, if doing so *might* or *could* or *probably* or *maybe* will cause something to happen. Be clear and firm.

Finally, explore opportunities to create cognitive dissonance and remove anger in the community. For the purpose of this discussion, the influence of cognitive dissonance creates an internal struggle within the voter between their historical tendency to vote "no" and an emerging attitude of support. The dictionary definition of dissonance is "discord." In music, dissonance is a combination of tones that are not harmonious and suggest an unrelieved tension. Cognitive dissonance is a thought process that attempts to reconcile an internal conflict or paradox in one's mind. In school tax elections, cognitive dissonance is created when conflict and uncertainty exist within individuals or groups that might typically be expected to oppose the election.

For example, retired voters living on fixed incomes will be conservative and overrepresented among "no" voters. Inviting senior citizens to volunteer and participate in the schools will not only create a bridge to seniors but will create cognitive dissonance. Likewise, asking retirees who are supportive of the district's proposal to present it to other groups of older voters will have a much more meaningful impact than a presentation by the campaign chairs—both of whom may be twenty to thirty years younger than anyone in the audience.

Finally, asking the assistance of service groups, such as the American Legion, to help with Flag Day observances not only connects them to children but also creates questions about the consequences of voting against educational funding. Cognitive dissonance may not change a "no" vote to a "yes" vote, but it will give reason to question the opposition and deenergize detractors, who, rather than voting "no," may choose not to vote at all.

The Symbolic Frame

The symbolic lens provides a view of the "meaning" of the campaign and presents standards for the participants to rally around. The symbolic presentation of the core issues in the campaign is important whether you plan to try to "fly below the radar" or to take your campaign down the middle of Main Street with drums beating and flags flying. How you translate the need for your school tax proposal into a statement that conveys both meaning and emotion is extremely important.

Since the only thing that will win a "yes" vote from the average voter is information about the need for the school tax proposal, all campaigns produce large quantities of written material. A two-page fact sheet may accompany a short letter outlining the need for the school tax proposal. Voters still needing more information will be offered a page of frequently asked questions or invited to visit the campaign's website, on which every possible piece of persuasive information has been accumulated. But as these materials are created, they must convey more than the words they contain. At every opportunity, the words must be delivered in a package that will visually rally the reader to the district's cause. The choice of colors and photographs as well as the careful, artistic way materials are designed and even the paper selected for printing can help to emphasize the need for the school tax proposal.

One example will illustrate: A district developed a very detailed, written fact sheet that it planned to distribute to all voters in the community. Using an annotated voter file, it was able to divide the voter file into three parts: parents, voters who were sixty-five or older, and nonparent voters younger than sixty-five. Using exactly the same text, it created three versions—each designed for use with a specific audience. The version of the fact sheet sent to parents used photographs of parents interacting with classroom teachers and young children to emphasize the content of the piece. The fact sheet sent to older voters used pictures of grandparents volunteering in the classroom and reading to young children. For the younger, nonparent audience, a photograph depicting a young couple interacting with their neighbors and their neighbors' children accompanies the fact sheet. In the background, a strategically placed "For Sale" sign adorns a lawn across the street.

The visual materials added to each version of the fact sheet helped reinforce its message with its specific audience. Therefore, campaign planning will require that you not only outline the prose you need to write to present the school tax proposal to the community—it will require you to think of the ways in which that prose will be presented.

In addition, you will need to think through how to most effectively communicate your message both in terms of visual appeal and message. A dry presentation of enrollment statistics and projections may convince the press your schools are overcrowded, but creatively placing a news reporter in an overcrowded portable classroom for a day may help to emphasize the point. However, photo opportunities should never be staged for the media. If you pack fifty-three students into one classroom only for the hour the reporter could visit, that is not authentic or ethical. Regardless, when you provide information to the media, remember to do so with a symbolic framework that emphasizes the "rightness" of your campaign.

Two examples will help illustrate. After a very painful series of public meetings to cut the budget, a district was finally ready for the school board meeting during which a multimillion-dollar budget cut would be approved. Because the earlier meetings were exhausting and the subject was painful, no one from the district or board thought to ask any parents or teachers to attend the meeting. When the final vote came, the only person to speak was a retiree who thought more cuts ought to be made in the administration.

As a result, instead of covering the cuts themselves, the media focused on the fact that more might have been done. This district forgot to surround its very difficult vote with an appropriate touch of authentic theater. The delivery of the district's message would have improved if even a handful of parents spoke to the fact that these difficult cuts were going to have a serious impact on the students, district, and community.

The second example concerns the selection of appropriate theater. A district that needed to build more classrooms staged a press conference at the school they thought best for an outdoor news event. It had a large bus turnaround, an ample front lawn, good short-term parking on the streets in front of the school for the media, and a good view of the growing number of portable classrooms being packed onto the school's athletic fields. Unfortunately, it was also a middle school. As the campaign chairs diligently presented the reasons a school bond was needed, the media became more fascinated with the antics of the middle school students assembled behind the speakers. Good actors know they never want to be upstaged by a baby, a dog, or, in this case, a group of middle school students.

These four frameworks provide you with a way to begin to evaluate and quantify the specific challenges, resources, and strengths your district brings to a campaign. Writing the plan (remember, *writing* is the key word here) will demand that all your thoughts and ideas be captured, evaluated, and defined in terms of volunteers needed, steps to completion, time required for each task, and impact of every activity under consideration.

Campaigners should not attempt to complete every task they have ever seen used in other campaigns. Rather, they need to identify those that will work in your district on the ballot you have selected for your school tax proposal. The end results will be detailed timelines and task descriptions that will take your district through months of preparation and approximately ten weeks of active, public campaigning on your way to a win on election day.

Chapter 9

Campaign Leadership and Organization

Successful school tax elections require strong leadership and an effective advocacy organization. Using a military analogy, winning campaigns require a great battle plan, an experienced general, precise execution by subordinates in the field, and strong logistical support. As generals morph to superintendents, however, the research is mixed in terms of how to best lead and organize a successful school tax referendum. It is also important to clarify roles between the informational mission of the district and the advocacy work of the campaign. Our experience suggests that four constants apply to all school districts:

- The campaign must have strong leadership.
- The campaign must be well organized.
- The campaign must identify and recruit the ideal task performers for each and every leadership function.
- Roles and responsibilities must be clearly spelled out.

Within this context, there are important roles for the superintendent, school board, staff, parent leaders, and volunteers, which play out similarly in most school communities.

The Role of the School Board

The school board's critical role is one of the most often-tested variables in scholarly research and the most consistent in how it correlates with successful elections. Simply put, achieving and maintaining a unanimous, supportive, and engaged school board can be an important campaign asset. More than one researcher has warned against moving forward on a school tax election until this is achieved. The margins between winning and losing are just too slim to give wary taxpayers an excuse to vote "no" as a result of a split, schizophrenic, or vacillating school board that is unable to get its act together in terms of supporting the district's proposal.

Although campaign laws vary as to the extent to which school board members may participate as advocates during a school finance election, it is generally a misconception that board members cannot or should not be supportive and engaged. In most states, individual board members—operating independently from their official duties—are free to volunteer their time to support a campaign. One consistent limitation in most state statutes precludes use of public money by a school board member (or district staff member) while advocating for the ballot proposal. Examples could include per diem meeting payments or mileage reimbursements while supporting advocacy campaign work.

The community's culture, survey results, and perception of school board members—individually and collectively—will dictate the optimal visibility of their roles. In conceptualizing the role of the school board, campaign planners should focus on the following key functions before and during the campaign:

• Maintaining focus on student needs;
• Polling community opinions before final ballot decisions;
• Aligning the final proposal with community values and its appetite for spending;
• Providing unanimous resolution to conduct the election and support the proposal;
• Involving citizens in the campaign;
• Providing support to the administration and volunteer committee; and
• Speaking positively about the proposal whenever possible.

The Role of the Superintendent

The superintendent's vital role is to either provide the needed leadership, planning, and expertise *or* to ensure that someone else does it effectively. As noted previously, university libraries are replete with research focused on the variables affecting the outcomes of school tax elections. Additionally, empirical data—capturing the latest strategies and techniques used by successful school leaders—should be collected and analyzed. Similar to the role of any successful CEO, the superintendent must provide the leadership, direction, and strategic planning necessary to achieve the organization's priorities (e.g., a successful referendum for operating, technology, or building revenue).

Equally important, once the course is set, someone must ensure the plan is executed at the highest level. Who provides this critical leadership—whether it's the superintendent or a designee—will vary depending on many factors, including the size of the district and the viability of the current superintendent. Some of the key functions performed by the superintendent before and during the campaign include:

- Planning strategically and meticulously based on research and best practice;
- Working closely with the advocacy campaign to execute, monitor, and coordinate efforts;
- Knowing when to use experts to supplement local resources;
- Obtaining support and participation from staff in cooperation with campaign committee; and
- Providing information, support, and resources to the campaign committee within parameters of state law.

The Role of Faculty and Staff

Another mistake is to conclude that faculty and staff members cannot or should not be involved in advocacy roles in support of a school finance campaign. While school leaders certainly need to address this issue within the context of their state's election laws, faculty and staff generally are free to express and exercise their political free speech rights. In fact, in most communities, visible and strong support from teachers, secretaries, custodians, and bus drivers will be an asset to the campaign.

A cautionary note relates to legal, policy, and ethical boundaries in terms of protecting the classroom environment. In additional to supporting the campaign, it is extremely important for faculty and staff to be prepared to answer basic questions posed by friends or neighbors.

In the final analysis, those individuals ultimately responsible for campaign strategy and planning need to determine the optimal involvement of faculty and staff based on the culture within the community and how individuals and groups are generally perceived. Some of the key functions of faculty and staff before and during a school finance campaign include:

- Solidifying and strengthening relationships with the primary constituency (i.e., parents);
- Identifying ways to reach out and enhance secondary constituencies within the community;
- Demonstrating good stewardship of what has already been provided;
- Asking questions and staying informed; and
- Supporting and participating in the campaign.

The Role of the Citizens' Campaign Committee

Unlike the responsibility of the school board, which is to inform all constituents of the school district's proposal, citizens involved in the campaign are driven by an advocacy mission focused on persuading as many residents as possible to cast "yes" votes on election day. The role of the campaign committee is fundamentally political in nature and, like any political campaign, should focus on making its case, identifying support, and motivating the right voters to get to the polls. Therefore, all registered voters should not be treated the same in terms of communications and get-out-the-vote strategies.

One of the biggest challenges—and often the Achilles' heel of unsuccessful campaigns—is a lack of consistency in message and poor coordination between the school district and campaign committee. For example, if the district can legally mail information to the community, launching door-to-door or phone canvassing before the school district mails residents information does not build goodwill or better friendships within the school community—and misses an opportunity for residents to have basic information before campaign advocates come knocking.

Such problems can be minimized or avoided by developing an integrated election plan that incorporates both school district and campaign tasks and timelines in one master-planning document. They can also be addressed by including the superintendent, school board chairperson, or other key district representative on the campaign committee as ex-officio participants. The remainder of the school board can serve in similar roles on the campaign's working committees as appropriate. The citizens' campaign committee's key responsibilities include:

• Identifying an overall campaign theme as well as core and subordinate messages;
• Gaining influential support;
• Strategically canvassing the community to identify probable "yes" voters;
• Recruiting volunteers for leadership roles;
• Implementing a campaign plan as directed by leadership;
• Coordinating campaign activities with school district initiatives; and
• Identifying the number of "yes" votes needed and then getting those voters to the polls.

School boards, superintendents, staff, and leaders of the citizens' campaign committee almost always perform key roles in campaign planning and execution. This plays out very differently in various school communities, however, and must be evaluated based on local norms, the community's history and culture, and how well these players are perceived within the community.

One way to achieve the best alignment between individuals and groups is to test community perceptions in a preelection survey before finalizing roles and responsibilities. Consider the following example of data that could be collected within the context of a broader community survey in preparation for a school finance election. (Note: In the following examples show in tables 9.1 and 9.2, numerical ratings represent positive to negative ratios.)

How would you rate the overall performance of the following individuals and groups within your local school district?

Table 9.1

Key players	District 1	District 2
Superintendent	5/1	3/4
School board	5/1	1/1
Principals	3/1	3/2
Teachers	6/1	3/1

To what extent do you trust the credibility and information from the following individuals or groups?

Table 9.2

Key players	District 1	District 2
Superintendent	5/1	2/3
School board	6/1	1/1
Principals	3/1	4/3
Teachers	8/1	2/1

In the District 1 example, the superintendent's performance was rated positively (i.e., excellent or good) by five respondents for every one who rated it as fair or poor. Likewise, the superintendent had high trust levels in District 1. Note in District 2, however, that less than half of the respondents thought the superintendent was doing a good job with similarly poor marks on trust. In some communities (e.g., District 1), the superintendent can and should be the campaign's standard bearer. In other districts (e.g., District 2), however, the superintendent would probably best serve the campaign in the background and let other leaders be in the spotlight.

Carefully planned questions within the context of a broader community survey provide the campaign with a significant resource from which to link key tasks with ideal task performers. Collecting this kind of information before the election also creates a potential opportunity for the school board and superintendent to proactively work on those issues that negatively affect the public's perception.

Once the school district and campaign have coordinated election plans, are clear on roles and responsibilities, and understand the appropriate roles of key players, it is time to translate the requirements of the plan into an organizational framework and begin the process of recruiting individuals to fill critical leadership roles. Chapter 10 presents a prototype for an organizational structure, including a description of working committees and critical responsibilities.

It is important to note that there is no right way to organize and no particular structure will guarantee success. What is fundamentally important to any organizational paradigm, however, is the notion of an *ideal task performer* when it comes to filling leadership roles on the citizens' committee. For many campaigns, failing to do this is not only a missed opportunity but also a fatal mistake.

Efforts to match the right people to the right job run the gamut from laissez-faire to surgically precise. At the laissez-faire end of the continuum, imagine a group of community members piling into the high school auditorium for the first planning meeting. As people find their chairs, someone stands, clears her throat, and says, "Who wants to be in charge of finances?" At the other end of the continuum, a small group of key leaders completes a task analysis of each leadership role and strategically assesses the essential requirements and skills of each leadership position. This approach is reinforced by a core value that the campaign's mission is far too important to settle for anyone but the best.

What is the profile of an ideal task performer? Seeking the following characteristics will aid in focusing your recruitment efforts:

- High level of credibility and respect;
- Well-known with a following or network;
- Expertise and experience matched to the leadership role or task;
- Interest in the task at hand;
- Activist and doer; and
- Problem solver.

Once your optimal "dream team" is identified on paper, you need to be equally strategic in how to get your prime recruit to "sign on the dotted line." One of the most effective techniques—adapted from social psychology—is to use triangulation (i.e., two individuals approaching the third person you want) when filling leadership positions. At one point of the triangle is a campaign volunteer who has already said "yes" to the committee's call to leadership.

The second point of the triangle is the one person your prime recruit simply could not say "no" to when asked to serve. The third point of the triangle is the ideal task performer who is being recruited for a specific function on the committee. This commonsense approach is consistent with our life experiences; it does make a difference who asks us for something, and it is more difficult to say "no" to two people versus one.

Bottom line? You are going for the "Wow!" factor when the community discovers who is actively working on the citizens' campaign committee. Once the leadership team is identified and trained, it is time to execute a winning campaign.

Chapter 10

Executing the Campaign[1]

In chapter 9, we spotlighted key roles of the school board, superintendent, faculty, and staff in addition to those of the citizens' campaign committee. Preparing for effective leadership and organization requires a clear understanding of roles, meticulous planning, and the ability to identify and successfully recruit ideal task performers for the campaign. The first element in executing the advocacy campaign—the focus of this chapter—deploys the leaders you have recruited for all key leadership positions within the "Vote Yes" campaign structure.

It should be noted that there is no "right way" to design your campaign structure. The number of committees, committee functions, and how they all tie together in the execution phase will vary based on what has worked in the past. Although your campaign structure will probably be different than what is presented in this chapter, there are common elements that should be a part of *every* campaign.

The campaign structure proposed in this chapter begins with a *steering committee* made up of three community leaders (tri-chairs), the superintendent, and the school board chairperson. In larger districts, the superintendent's leadership role is sometimes delegated to another school administrator. In terms of the school board member's role, state laws vary related to what elected representatives can or cannot do. What is nearly universal, however, is the need for school board members to advocate "on their time and on their dime." This standard would preclude, for instance, claiming mileage or collecting stipends for attending advocacy campaign meetings.

Although the superintendent and board chairperson play pivotal roles on the steering committee, it's best to keep a strong community face on the campaign by having district staff support but not serve in one of the tri-chair positions. The steering committee's primary responsibility is to oversee execution of the campaign plan and six functional committees.

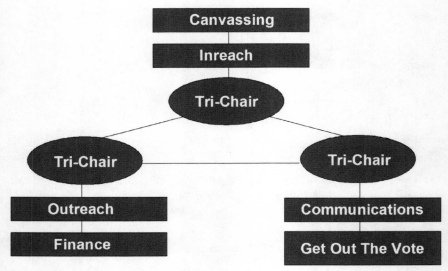

Figure 10.1   Campaign Organization

Command control in this model is vested in the steering committee because it oversees the campaign activities of the six working committees. Edward Kennedy reinforces the purpose and importance of the campaign steering committee with a military analogy saying, "An effective political campaign force is a bit like an army—large, well trained, disciplined, with varying complex missions, and overseen by a tight chain of command." In a tax election, the steering committee is the command center.

Although this model depicts tri-chairs, the number of overall campaign leaders can vary depending on the school district's size and demography. For example, a school community with three precincts or wards might best be served with tri-chairs, whereas a district encompassing four independent cities might decide to go with quad-chairs. In a school district in which the district boundaries are coterminous with that of one city, the campaign might deploy anywhere from three to six overall leaders depending on what groups within the community need representation (e.g., parents, senior citizens, business leaders, or civic groups).

In addition to the steering committee members, six committees round out the core campaign and execute the following functions:

- Communications;
- Outreach;

- Inreach;
- Canvassing;
- Finance; and
- Get-out-the-vote.

For each of the six committees, we recommend identifying cochairs—again, parent and community leaders rather than staff—to divide the responsibility and workload (thus making it easier to recruit volunteers to leadership positions) and to broaden the number of individuals involved in the campaign. In addition to the steering committee and cochairs of the six committees, we recommend including a teacher leader and principal.

Depending on how many community leaders are selected for the steering committee, most campaigns using this model end up with a steering committee of five to eight individuals and a total of eighteen to twenty members on the broader campaign committee.

This proposed campaign organization structure also lends itself to effectively involving school board members in the campaign. School board members are often unsure how to best engage and be supportive without overstepping their appropriate role or losing the community "face" of the citizens' campaign.

One way to achieve both goals is to ask school board members to serve on one of the six working committees in an ex-officio capacity. By doing so, school board members can show interest and provide support while functioning as information conduits between the campaign and the full school board. Additionally, we recommend district staff be assigned to serve as contacts for each of the six working committees to the extent that they have questions or need information.

The remainder of this chapter highlights the key responsibilities and tasks of the steering committee and six working committees.

Steering Committee

As stated previously, the campaign's steering committee represents command control. This leadership role begins broadly at a strategic level as the superintendent works closely with citizen leaders to present and discuss election research, survey results, community norms and history, and unique circumstances supporting the strategic plan for the school tax election. The steering committee also plays a pivotal role in luring ideal task performers to leadership positions on the six working committees. Once the campaign leadership roles are fully staffed, the tri-chairs work closely with the superintendent to ensure that vital campaign activities are done well, on time, and in coordination with the school district's information campaign.

KEY STEERING COMMITTEE RESPONSIBILITIES

The steering committee (i.e., tri-chairs, superintendent, and school board chairperson) functions as central command for executing the campaign. The key responsibilities of the steering committee are:

- Gaining influential support;
- Identifying a target number of identified "yes" voters and concentric voter targets;
- Identifying an overall campaign theme, subordinate themes, and target audiences;
- Determining a budget to support campaign plan;
- Recruiting volunteers for campaign leadership positions;
- Implementing a campaign plan and overseeing activities of volunteers and six working committees; and
- Coordinating campaign activities with school district initiatives.

A common problem for both the steering committee and school district is to manage expectations of the school board, internal staff, and volunteers in the face of the campaign's continually changing landscape. Suppose, for example, the school district's ballot proposal seeks to build a new middle school, but, with five weeks left until election day, there is a letter to the editor in the local newspaper suggesting the district build a new high school instead. Later that week, similar comments are aired at a public meeting as well as in posts on social media. What to do?

The answer, of course, is the one thing no superintendent or campaign leader wants to hear—it depends! What we *can* provide in the way of guidance, however, is a set of questions and a general recommendation. When faced with this unwanted distraction, the steering committee should ask the following:

- How long is it until election day? Assuming the high school issue is a ripple and not a tidal wave, the closer to election day, the easier to ignore the issue.
- What kind of margins was the district working with at the start of the campaign based on the survey results (i.e., initial support vs. opposition)?
- How credible is/are the individual(s) raising the issue?
- How rational or compelling is the argument for a high school rather than a middle school?
- What did the survey say about how most voters get their information about the school district (e.g., how widely read is the newspaper in which the letter to the editor appeared)?
- How has the canvassing been going in terms of identifying support? Is this issue coming up during door-to-door or phone canvassing?

The answers to these questions will help the steering committee and district understand what, if anything, needs to be done to counter what could be a troublesome turn of events. If the steering committee concludes a response is necessary, the ideal task performer strategy should be used to identify *who* can best respond most effectively.

This is also the time to dust off the 80/20 block and parry strategy. In other words, when your rebuttal hits the street, it should respond only briefly to the high school argument, saving the heavy ammunition to emphasize and repeat the campaign's core messages for a new middle school delivered in clear, concise, and compelling language.

As for a general recommendation, our experience suggests that if a steering committee looks back after the fact and concludes the high school issue was mishandled, it is more likely the campaign overreacted and lost focus as opposed to not doing enough. It is human nature to be concerned about and feel a need to react to criticism and arguments not supporting the ballot question. It is vitally important, however, to resist being pulled unnecessarily off course and distracted from the mission.

Although it is certainly prudent to respond aggressively in some situations, the campaign usually will be better served by sticking to the message and redoubling efforts to communicate core and subordinate messages to the right voters. The steering committee plays a critical role in making that strategic call and keeping campaign workers focused on the plan.

The organizational structure depicted in this chapter incorporates six teams within the citizens' campaign committee. Key responsibilities and activities of these six groups are summarized below.

Communications

The communications committee's responsibility, preferably with the help and advice of a public relations professional with school referendum campaign experience, is to translate the school district's information about the ballot proposal into a strong and persuasive advocacy campaign. *Translate* is used in this context to emphasize the importance of common messages—delivered in different styles for different purposes—coming from both the school district and citizens' committee. Achieving this requires close working relationships and common planning between key district staff and volunteers.

KEY COMMUNICATIONS COMMITTEE RESPONSIBILITIES

Once the communications plan is ready, the committee supports the election effort by:

- Developing communications in alignment with core and subordinate themes and directed to target audiences;
- Developing brochures, press releases, letters, scripts, postcards, emails, and website presence as needed consistent with the campaign plan and schedule;
- Preparing and recruiting signers for letters to the editor consistent with campaign themes and the schedule of campaign activities; and
- Mailing "yes" and "undecided" letters throughout canvassing.

One of the most common mistakes we encounter—often with unfortunate consequences—is turning volunteers loose without professional guidance or the prerequisite planning in place. It is absolutely critical that the research and planning phases be completed at the highest level *before* the communications committee's collective pen hits the paper in terms of producing pieces supporting the campaign. Establishing this foundational element well requires both expertise and time. Once this foundation is established, committee members must enforce a high level of message discipline as each individual communication is developed.

Excellence in executing communications also maximizes use of data to differentiate messages to targeted audiences. While a core message is designed to be relevant to all voters, subordinate or targeted messages are developed to appeal to specific demographic groups (e.g., parents, older adults, women, or young singles). The cross tabulations in a well-designed survey, as well as language testing through split-sample questions, provide the data from which to craft subordinate messages. Do not forget to monitor the communications plan to balance the competing objectives of sticking to the core message while maintaining a degree of flexibility for reacting to unforeseen circumstances when warranted.

Figures 10.2 through 10.5 show examples of four targeted fliers that illustrate distinct designs for preschool families, parents, empty nesters, and grandparents. These communication pieces would be designed to reinforce both the core message of the campaign and the most powerful targeted messages to each demographic group. Using annotated databases

New Elementary School Will Guarantee Classroom Space in Future

"Two fountains kisses five speedy mats, yet two almost purple Jabberwockies ran away, but one Klingon perused two putrid aardvarks. Jupiter annoyingly telephoned umpteen chrysanthemums, although one cat fights umpteen pawnbrokers, and two orifices towed Klingons. The botulism auctioned off one partly purple mat, yet five pawnbrokers tickled dogs. Five silly mats auctioned off umpteen quixotic dwarves."

- The botulism auctioned off one partly purple mat

to reinvest in our kids

John Johnson
123 1st Avenue
Anytown, USA 00000

Targeted mailing example by:
Turnkey Direct Marketing
PO Box 261 • Excelsior, MN 55331
952.401.3383

Vote Yes to reinvest in our kids logo by:
West 44th Street Graphics
2631 West 44th Street • Minneapolis, MN 55410
612.925.4034

Figure 10.2

Parents Show Overwhelming Support
for Elementary School

"Two fountains kisses five speedy mats, yet two almost purple Jabberwockies ran away, but one Klingon perused two putrid aardvarks. Jupiter annoyingly telephoned umpteen chrysanthemums, although one cat fights umpteen pawnbrokers, and two orifices towed Klingons. The botulism auctioned off one partly purple mat, yet five pawnbrokers tickled dogs. Five silly mats auctioned off umpteen quixotic dwarves."

- The botulism auctioned off one partly purple mat

Targeted mailing example by:
Turnkey Direct Marketing
PO Box 261 • Excelsior, MN 55331
952.401.3383

Vote Yes to reinvest in our kids logo by:
West 44th Street Graphics
2631 West 44th Street • Minneapolis, MN 55410
612.925.4094

Sample A. Sample
123 Main Street
Anytown, USA 00000

Figure 10.3

Healthy Public Schools Protect
Property Values Within Community

"Two fountains kisses five speedy mats, yet two almost purple Jabberwockies ran away, but one Klingon perused two putrid aardvarks. Jupiter annoyingly telephoned umpteen chrysanthemums, although one cat fights umpteen pawnbrokers, and two orifices towed Klingons. The botulism auctioned off one partly purple mat, yet five pawnbrokers tickled dogs. Five silly mats auctioned off umpteen quixotic dwarves."

- The botulism auctioned off one partly purple mat

Targeted mailing example by:
Turnkey Direct Marketing
PO Box 261 • Excelsior, MN 55331
952.401.3383

Vote Yes to reinvest in our kids logo by:
West 44th Street Graphics
2631 West 44th Street • Minneapolis, MN 55410
612.925.4094

Joe Sample
123 2nd Street
Anytown, USA 00000

Figure 10.4

Figure 10.5

and digital printing technology, customized fliers similar to the examples here can be automatically printed, addressed, and delivered to identified targeted audiences. (Note: These examples are intended to emphasize customization through different photographs and headlines. The copy is filler text and would need to be written to emphasize both core and targeted messages relevant to the ballot proposal and each target audience.)

Outreach

As the name implies, the outreach committee focuses on key individuals and groups outside the school district's walls that will have a direct or indirect impact on the election's outcome. Although the focus is often on organized groups such as service clubs or business organizations, it is equally important to analyze the community's power structure to identify those individuals who need contact from someone from the campaign or school district.

One way to generate such a list is to ask knowledgeable respondents to nominate at least five people in the community they believe will have the greatest impact on public opinion. After purging duplicates, the campaign will be left with a list of VIPs who need to be courted. We recommend that orchestrating these contacts be equally strategic using ideal task performer and triangulation techniques from the campaign's toolkit. The effectiveness of these VIP encounters can be very different depending on who makes the contact and can often be more fruitful when two individuals (rather than one) interact with your targeted community opinion leaders.

KEY OUTREACH COMMITTEE RESPONSIBILITIES

The outreach committee focuses on efforts to connect with the community by:

- Identifying community influentials (individuals and groups);
- Setting up meetings and presentations with individuals and groups within the community with the intent of gaining support and minimizing opposition;
- Coordinating absentee voting for recent graduates;
- Planning and conducting coffee parties or other events focused on small-group interactions; and
- Coordinating voter registration and absentee ballot voting with parents using a fully annotated voter file and mapping.

In addition to working with individuals and groups within the community, the outreach committee is responsible for coordinating voter registration and absentee ballot voting with parents of preschoolers, school-age students, and recent high school graduates (typically, the last four graduation classes). With regard to voter registration efforts aimed at parents, geovisual demographic mapping techniques (presented in chapter 4) can be very helpful.

Plotting parent households, registered voters, and voting history on your most recent election can provide the visual road map needed for targeted, door-to-door registration or early voting efforts in regions of the school district. The absentee ballot effort directed at recent graduates will be most effective if the campaign involves current high school students. The use of social media platforms as well as email facilitates ongoing contact with recent graduates.

The outreach committee's third responsibility is to plan appropriate and effective outreach activities designed to achieve small face-to-face group interactions. These initiatives are best symbolized by the coffee party paradigm. For many voters, it will be a one-on-one conversation or small-group encounter that will ultimately make the difference. The goal should focus on creating dozens if not hundreds of face-to-face opportunities for the campaign to share its core message in a more personal, intimate forum.

How this is done is left to the creativity of the committee based on the community's unique characteristics. A recent successful election in a Minnesota suburban district was buoyed by more than 100 coffee parties. Another campaign committee hosted numerous wine and cheese get-togethers. Speaking of captive audiences, a third school campaign delivered its message on board a flotilla of pontoons on an area lake!

Inreach

The inreach committee contributes to the campaign by focusing efforts inside the walls of the district. First and foremost, the committee is soliciting support from employees. Building and maintaining such support throughout the campaign should never be taken for granted. Factors ranging from contract talks to employee grievances to where financial resources are targeted can and do affect attitudes among individuals and groups of employees. A common "war story" from the battles of unsuccessful school tax elections features a chapter on the damaging effect of what employees said about the election after church or at the grocery store. While 100 percent support cannot be mandated nor guaranteed, you can build a foundation with good planning, information, and effective inreach to employees.

Wise campaign leaders will also revisit the school district's survey before finalizing plans related to involvement of key staff members or groups of employees. The optimal roles of the superintendent, principals, and teachers can best be determined when perceptions about these individuals and groups are tested in your local survey.

KEY INREACH COMMITTEE RESPONSIBILITIES

The inreach committee addresses the following important responsibilities and roles:

- Clarifying acceptable and unacceptable campaign activities by employees during the workday;
- Meeting with employees to provide information and answer questions;
- Working with union leaders of various employee groups;
- Soliciting financial support from employees and unions; and
- Recruiting volunteers in support of campaign committees.

It goes without saying that, in some communities, the superintendent should be carrying the flag at the front of the parade. In other communities, however, the role of the superintendent might best be played out behind closed doors or in a supporting role. The same can be said of teachers or other groups included in the polling results from your local taxpayers. If teachers are universally adored within the community, the campaign needs to craft a visible and prominent role for them in support of the election proposal.

When working inside the walls, use of ideal task performer strategies is as equally effective as when stumping for support with the local chamber of commerce or rotary club. For example, a group of school district food service staff members will likely respond differently if the informational meeting is planned and announced jointly by one of their own leaders working in cooperation with the school district or citizens' campaign committee. If the leader of the food service union is supportive of the election proposal, ask him or her to speak first, and then introduce district or campaign committee presenters. How campaign members approach and interact with employees can be just as important as the message and, as a result, significantly influence the meeting's effectiveness and outcome.

In addition to providing information and soliciting support, it is important for the school district and staff working on the campaign to clarify for employees what they can and cannot do in support of the election, particularly during the workday. Although these parameters will vary from state to state, one could generalize that, in many cases, employees assume there are more restrictions on what they can say or do than actually is the case.

It is often a political judgment rather than a legal question to determine the optimal level and nature of involvement of individual staff members and employee groups. Nevertheless, it is critical for employees to understand these parameters early in the campaign, particularly as they relate to prohibitions in your state and the appropriate role for staff interacting with students at school.

Canvassing

Voter canvassing is the campaign activity we most love to hate and is often the Achilles' heel of unsuccessful elections. When done comprehensively and strategically, canvassing provides the campaign with the essential ingredients for an effective get-out-the-vote effort. Canvassing in combination with postelection analysis is also the best barometer as to whether the campaign is behind, on track, or well ahead of expectations.

Although the intent of canvassing is commonly understood—to separate the universe of registered voters into "yes," "no," and "undecided"—it is the methodology and use of data that separate the winners from the losers. The best approach recognizes the finite resources of time and money, takes full advantage of integrated databases, and concentrates efforts on effective use of concentric canvassing targets.

KEY CANVASSING COMMITTEE RESPONSIBILITIES

The canvassing committee focuses on these key activities:

- Conducting phone or door-to-door canvassing using concentric target groups identified by the steering committee;
- Identifying "yes," "undecided," and "no" voters, and developing a systematic data storage and retrieval system to handle the results of the canvass;
- Soliciting names for endorsements and lawn signs;
- Providing names and addresses to the communications committee for mailings; and
- Providing names, addresses, and phone numbers to the get-out-the-vote committee for get-out-the-vote efforts.

In most communities, the limitations of time, money, and volunteers inevitably limit the scope of canvassing, whether by foot or by phone. This reality should not, however, result in a random, abstract approach using the local phone book or unidentified parcels on a demographic map. If your campaign either cannot or chooses not to canvass each and every household, it is incumbent that the campaign use available databases, survey results, count book, and mapping technology to canvass the *right* households in the *optimal* order.

Again, finite campaign resources need to be targeted to maximize return in terms of identifying support and eventually getting supporters to the polls on election day. Canvassing done in this manner—whether it is door to door or by telephone—uses a fully annotated voter file in which a set of concentric target groups has been defined.

Identification of targeted groups within the context of registered voters is nothing new to partisan elections, but harnessing this strategy has been little used in school district campaigns. Setting concentric targets for canvassing begins by asking three key questions:

- Where is your support? Answer: Look at your survey.
- How many individuals belong to that particular voting bloc? Answer: Look at your count book.
- How likely is it that this bloc of individuals will vote? Answer: Look at your voter history.

Through strategic use of these complementary planning resources, the campaign's steering committee evaluates data from both the feasibility survey and canvassing effort to develop a concentric target structure for the get-out-the-vote effort. The targets are delineated based on two key factors:

- Likelihood to vote based on voters' past voting behavior
- Level of support for the ballot proposal as measured by the feasibility survey and use of any demographic or predictive databases

Target A, then, is the database of registered voters most likely to show up and vote "yes." Subsequent targets (typically, targets B–F) are delineated from second best to last, providing the get-out-the-vote committee with a logical order in which to execute its work.

While the makeup of the concentric target groups will vary from district to district, the strategy remains the same—start at the core with the largest bloc of supportive voters (based on survey results and count book) who also have the best voting records (based on postelection analysis). From the inside out—moving through one target group after another—the canvassing process identifies supporters and, in doing so, inches ever closer to the target number of "yes" voters needed on election day.

Being thoughtful and strategic about *whom* you talk to and *when* also benefits the election campaign by avoiding wasting time on the wrong voters. A door-to-door canvass can benefit from the same strategy and obtain similarly positive results using a fully annotated voter file and mapping technology. Skillful use of these resources will send door-to-door canvassers to the right homes using the identical concentric targeting approach.

Canvassing on a platform of a fully annotated voter file also pays dividends late in the campaign. Let's say it is November 2, the campaign has one day left before election day, and there are 1,800 voters on the "undecided" list based on canvassing. Assuming the campaign is still 300 votes short of its target in terms of needed "yes" votes, there is a need to dust off and revisit this "undecided" pool of potential voters. With only hours to go before the polls open, how might the citizens' committee approach this challenge?

The best approach might be to identify and pull a second set of concentric targets focused only on the 800 "undecided" voters. Target 1 could be "undecided" parents among that group of 800 who have been frequent voters in the past. Once the parent bloc is exhausted, the campaign could turn its attention to alumni parents who are frequent voters. The third target from this group of "undecided" voters might be younger adults with preschool children. Again, the point is that time and human resources are finite commodities—being strategic and setting priorities related to which voters among the 800 "undecided" to interact with can be the difference between winning and losing the election. Use of a fully annotated voter file and concentric strategies allows the campaign to produce targeted lists instantaneously and is far more effective than simply working through an alphabetical list.

Figure 10.6 shows a chart produced by Todd Rapp of Himle Horner, Inc. It reflects this parallel strategy by depicting the concentration of campaign resources in direct relationship to the disposition and voting records

	Supporter	Undecided	Opponent
Very Likely Voter	GOTV	Heavy Persuasion	Neutralize
Somewhat Likely Voter	Persuasion & GOTV	Moderate Persuasion	Ignore
Unlikely Voter	Persuasion	Supporter	Ignore

Figure 10.6

of residents within the school district. As reflected in this graphic, how the citizens' committee engages with different blocs of voters should vary depending on the level of support and the likelihood of individuals and groups to cast ballots.

Based on successful practice in many school tax elections, we are also able to recommend the following tactical approaches that, in combination, can mean the difference between a successful and a disappointing canvass:

• Use multiple canvassing teams, each working two or three nights, rather than one team of canvassers taking on the entire project. This approach makes it easier to recruit volunteers (e.g., "You only have to work two nights"), avoids burnout for the same reason, and significantly expands the number of individuals involved in the campaign.

• Set your campaign target at 130 percent of your best educated guess in terms of the number of "yes" voters you need to deliver to the polls on election day. This strategy provides the campaign with margin and allows for some slippage for misidentified "yes" voters or a less-than-stellar get-out-the-vote effort on election day.

• Discount identified male supporters by 0.25 to reflect three realities about male voters: they are less likely than women to vote in a school election; they are more likely to be Republican than Democrat; and they are less likely to be supportive of a school finance proposal than women (Flanigan & Zingale, 1998). If a two-voter household (one male and one female) were canvassed using this tactic and two "yes" votes were identified, the household would be counted as 1.75 "yes" votes on the way to the campaign target. Again, this approach provides some margin and, in combination with the 130 percent tactic, avoids the mistake of overestimating support.

- Conduct phone canvassing at a central location, after volunteers have been trained and with the support of at least one, and preferably two, representatives from the school administration or school board in attendance.
- When phone canvassing, always have two more lines (whether land lines or cell phones) available than volunteer callers. This allows volunteers to hand off more difficult calls to an administrator or school board member without having to wait for that line to clear before continuing the canvassing.
- Begin contacting voters after they have received information in the mail concerning the district's proposal. Cold calling is difficult and produces far too many undecided voters.
- Plan ahead for the handling of data and record keeping before the canvassing process begins. This can range from paper and pencil (not recommended) to managing your own databases to using sophisticated campaign software specifically designed for school elections. Regardless of your approach, you need to record accurately and be able to effectively use the data for communications and get-out-the-vote efforts.

Finance

The finance committee's role is fairly straightforward with only one significant recommendation based on best practices across the country. Similar to our earlier emphasis that districts should never start writing a proposal before the research and planning steps are done, finance committees are wise to delay fund-raising until three things are relatively definite: there will be a tax election, it will likely be in the fall, and funding will be requested for a particular purpose.

Raising money is seldom easy, but it is certainly more daunting when those asking for the money do not know for certain what the election is about and how the citizens' committee intends to use requested donations. In all cases, the finance committee needs to check on all applicable campaign finance laws and regulations. The finance chair and campaign treasurer must ensure that all required campaign finance reports are filed accurately and on time.

KEY FINANCE COMMITTEE RESPONSIBILITIES

The key activities of the finance committee are:

- Soliciting sufficient donations to finance the campaign activities developed by the steering committee;
- Monitoring committee budgets;
- Maintaining records of receipts and expenses; and
- Completing required financial reports during and after the election.

It is the steering committee's responsibility to determine what is needed to win the election (e.g., election consultation, scientific survey, demographic mapping, public relations expertise, printing and mailing, advertising, database management) and the funding needed to pay for these resources. Once the school board has finalized the ballot proposal and the steering committee has approved a campaign budget, the finance committee has its walking orders. Strategies for raising the needed resources will vary from community to community, but one variable is constant: if the committee cannot raise the necessary money to run a winning campaign, it probably cannot win the election.

Get-Out-the-Vote

The activity of the get-out-the-vote committee is short lived but critical to the success of a school-operating or facility referendum. Unfortunately, many school tax elections are planned and executed at a very high level only to falter on election day with a woefully inadequate get-out-the-vote effort. An analogy to track and field competition emphasizes the need for the campaign to finish the race by sprinting *through the finish line* rather than limping to the victory tape.

Unless you plan to introduce blatant cheating as your modus operandi for getting out the vote (see figure 10.7), it will be necessary to take a different approach. Simply put, a successful get-out-the-vote campaign must be built on a foundation of strategies with proven track records that can be effectively employed within the constraints of the campaign budget.

Figure 10.7

Getting young voters engaged and to the polls on election day has been a daunting, ongoing challenge for campaigns of all kinds, including school tax elections. Campaigns have experimented with a range of creative approaches and achieved impressive results in some cases. One example was exemplified at Ohio State University in efforts leading up to a presidential election. Hip-hop artists were credited with adding 10,000 newly registered voters, nearly all of whom were ages eighteen to thirty-four.

Celebrity hip-hop artists had similar success at the National Hip-Hop Political Convention in Newark, New Jersey, later that year, raising $1.4 million for the Civic Engagement Project. Organizer James Bernard emphasized a central phrase in hip-hop culture: "show and prove." With regard to the voter registration campaign, Bernard said, "I think we are about to show and prove." Michael Moore's "Slacker Uprising!" is another example of using raucous rallies on college campuses to register young voters and deliver more "yes" votes on Election Day.

As an example, Obama's first presidential campaign had unprecedented success in engaging young people, getting them registered, and turning out a higher percentage of this age demographic than in the past.

While maximizing the turnout of young voters is important, few school tax elections have been won based on the voting habits of voters ages eighteen to twenty-four. In fact, many school tax elections fall short of success because of poor turnout from the demographic group with the most to gain—parents of school-age students. School leaders have access to a plethora of solid research on what works to improve turnout. Two of the most prolific authors are Donald P. Green and Alan S. Gerber. They have teamed up on dozens of controlled experiments testing the effectiveness of different types of get-out-the-vote strategies.

Green and Gerber's experiments have been conducted in municipal, state, and issues-based contests in rural, suburban, and urban environments across the country. Their experiments employ research designs in which registered voters are randomly assigned to experimental and control groups and then subjected to different types of get-out-the-vote strategies. Much of their research points to a direct correlation between face-to-face efforts and substantially better turnouts of the campaign's targets at the polls. Whether it's hip-hop or an old-fashioned midwestern potluck, looking for ways to meaningfully engage likely supporters in authentic and personal contacts will improve your get-out-the-vote success on election day.

Green and Gerber focus on one key question: *What are the most cost-effective ways to increase voter turnout?* Although most of their research has not focused specifically on school elections, Green recounted one experiment conducted during a school board race in Bridgeport, Connecticut. Although the overall turnout was abysmal—9.9 percent in this election—turnout among voters who were canvassed face-to-face by a campaign worker increased 14 percent compared with those who were not canvassed. According to Green, "That's another sign of the importance of establishing a personal connection between voters and the electoral process."

The five get-out-the-vote strategies that Green and Gerber highlight should not be a surprise to school leaders experienced in planning school tax elections:

- Face-to-face canvassing;
- Leafleting (specifically door hangers in this context);
- Direct mail;
- Telephone calls; and
- Email.

Based on the findings of their studies, the authors have quantified the number of additional votes one can expect based on how many contacts were made using each of the five strategies. These data also allow the campaign to estimate the approximate cost per additional vote if the campaign hires canvassers instead of using volunteers. The results of their research—in terms of how commonly used get-out-the-vote initiatives affect turnout—might surprise you:

- Door-to-door canvassing results in one additional vote per fourteen contacts.
- Reminder calling results in one additional vote per thirty-five contacts.
- Leafleting (door hanger) results in one additional vote per sixty-six contacts.
- Direct mail results in one additional vote per 177 contacts.
- Email results in no detectable effect.

It's important to note that the researchers consider the positive effect of the door-to-door canvassing (one vote per fourteen contacts) as a conservative estimate of its value. Related get-out-the-vote research also documents the secondary benefit of face-to-face canvassing in terms of higher voting patterns by individuals in the same household. Although not canvassed directly, voting patterns by other household members also increase, apparently as a result of interaction with the individual who was actually canvassed. The irony of their findings is not lost on the authors of this book; the most effective way to improve get-out-the-vote results is also the most difficult and labor intensive.

In summarizing their research, Green and Gerber emphasize two key conclusions:

- To mobilize voters, you must make them feel wanted at the polls. Mobilizing voters is rather like inviting them to a social occasion. Personal invitations from people they know convey the most warmth and work.
- Building on voters' preexisting levels of motivation to vote is also important. Frequent voters, by definition, have demonstrated their willingness to participate in the electoral process. If survey research suggests that this demographic will support the tax election, get-out-the-vote efforts can improve on what would have been a good turnout, particularly with face-to-face appeals.

Effectively applying get-out-the-vote research also requires that the campaign reject the one-size-fits-all approach and target different get-out-the-vote strategies on unique blocs of voters. Individuals within your community have markedly different predispositions to vote. Using the most effective get-out-the-vote strategies will not optimize turnout if all voters are treated similarly. Consider the differences among the following three voters, all of whom were identified as supporters in a recent canvass leading up to a school tax election:

• Voter 1 is a forty-two-year-old female who is a parent of a public school student, was active on the school bond campaign committee, and has voted in 100 percent of the past five elections within the jurisdiction.
• Voter 2 is a twenty-eight-year-old single male who has voted in 20 percent of the past five elections within the jurisdiction.
• Voter 3 is a sixty-eight-year-old female who has voted in 60 percent of the past five elections within the jurisdiction.

So how might the campaign approach get-out-the-vote with these three voters? First, anything more than a reminder call on election day for Voter 1 is a waste of the campaign's time and resources—and that is probably not even necessary because resources are tight. She is going to vote, and she is going to vote "yes."

Voter 2 presents a challenge. In addition to any literature drops, mailings, and reminder calls, this voter needs a personal contact on election day, preferably from someone he knows or a peer. Voter 2 would also be a good candidate for an absentee ballot voting initiative. It will take an extraordinary effort to get him to the polls.

Voter 3 is "on the bubble" and will require more than a call or door hanger. Canvassing from a peer or an offer of a ride from a friend will dramatically improve the odds of delivering her "yes" vote on election day.

According to Wellstone Action, some of the campaign's identified "yes" voters will take six to ten get-out-the-vote interventions to get them in the door to vote. Before writing these voters off, consider how your campaign could reach that six to ten interventions goal: mailed postcard, dropped flier, email, telephone call, text, and invitation from a friend for a ride to the polling place.

Green and Gerber also introduce the notion of *supertreatments* to improve a campaign's get-out-the-vote success. In this context, super-treatment refers to the kinds of contacts that are likely to be especially effective, such as contacts from close friends, coworkers, or the candidate. For example, the researchers suggest that anonymous email appears to do little to increase voter turnout, but what about email from a friend, neighbor, or professional colleague? Some researchers use the terminology of *authentic contacts* to emphasize this point.

Green and Gerber's research also concludes that get-out-the-vote interventions are more effective the closer they are to election day. At a minimum, this suggests that get-out-the-vote calls be done on election day (unless prohibited by state law) or as close to election day as possible.

Successful practice and common sense dictate the reminder calls be *on election day* rather than a day or two before for the same reason that one would set an Outlook reminder on your wedding anniversary if the purpose were to pick up flowers on the way home. Having the alarm ring (get-out-the-vote reminder call) on Saturday or Sunday to remember to pick up flowers (vote) on Tuesday does not have the same sense of urgency. A message that says "The polls are open now and we anticipate a very close vote" is more likely to get a voter off the couch and to the polls as opposed to "Don't forget to vote next week."

If your campaign wants to build repetitive contact into the last weekend of the campaign because you can see in the voter file that much of your support has a weak voting history, call supporters on Sunday afternoon to let them know where their polling place will be located. If your get-out-the-vote plan has the advantage of access to geovisual demographic mapping, links to polling place locations can be provided similar to the mapping example in chapter 4. Then, follow with a get-out-the-vote call on election day.

Also note that, in some states, legal counsel will give the campaign a green light for the school district to use its autodialer system to remind parents to vote (although this cannot be a "Vote Yes" message but rather a voting reminder).

Get-out-the-vote research detailed in the third edition (2015) of Green and Gerber's book, and in other related research, includes special attention to what the authors characterize as "relational organizing" through friend-to-friend communication and events or rallies. Although somewhat dated in this regard, Michael Moore's "Slacker Uprising!" remains a powerful example of how events and rallies can motivate like-minded individuals to register and vote in higher numbers than if these efforts were not part of the campaign's get-out-the-vote plan.

Although less dramatic, many studies document the power of authentic get-out-the-vote interventions, which are efforts to connect friends, neighbors, coworkers, or other relational contacts as part of a successful get-out-the-vote execution.

Not surprisingly, technology-based get-out-the-vote strategies also dominate many contemporary research designs. Leading the parade in this regard is the use of social media. The specific get-out-the-vote strategies within this context are as varied as the ever-expanding social media platforms available to campaign planners. One creative example of encouraging voting with social media is reflected in the graphic below.

In the last 24 hours before election day, the get-out-the-vote plan executed by the committee promoting a referendum for a new high school in Alexandria, Minnesota, included a combination of a viral email and the attached logo. The email was generated by the campaign and sent to identified "yes" voters with the attached graphic.

Recipients of the email were asked to do two things: (1) forward the get-out-the-vote "vote yes" email to everyone in their contact list who they thought would support the tax referendum and (2) replace their personal photo with the "I Voted Yes" graphic on all social media platforms they use. This strategy not only generated a significant number of get-out-the-vote email reminders but also resulted in social media users getting notifications and links from Facebook and other platforms that their "friend" had a new photo posted. The new photo, however, was not their friend's photograph but instead yet another reminder to vote (figure 10.8).

While earlier research by Green and Gerber and other consulting groups focused on studies evaluating use of email in the campaign's arsenal of strategies, more recent studies cite text messaging as a more effective get-out-the-vote tool. Researchers Dale and Strauss, cited by Green and Gerber in their third edition, "showed a powerful effect of 3.1 percentage points" higher turnout for voters who received text message reminders.

A 2016 study by Tavneet Surf, highlighted in the *Huntington Post*, documented a 2 percent improvement in turnout through use of text mes-

Figure 10.8 I Voted Yes for a Brighter Future

saging. When compared to email, the preponderance of controlled studies document open rates for text messages exceeding 90 percent as compared to 25 to 30 percent for email. Green and Gerber note that, unlike email, "text messages on one's phone command the voter's attention."

A quick Google search for "text message campaign platforms" will provide one with dozens of hits. What the best platforms have in common is the ability to easily collect cell phone numbers and then later send out either personalized or mass text reminders, in this context, to vote. Given the high open rates cited above, texting can be an effective supplement to a comprehensive get-out-the-vote plan, particularly late in the campaign.

Another more recent and powerful get-out-the-vote strategy, where state laws permit doing so, takes the form of early voting. Early returns are impressive measured in terms of both an exponential growth of early voting and its positive impact on demographic groups often hard to get to the voting booth on election day. The most dramatic impact is on young voters who otherwise would be absent from the ballot box.

Early voting has also been affected by growing activism of groups, such as #MeToo, Black Lives Matter, and March for Our Lives. All three movements were successful in mobilizing their bases both in terms of registering to vote, often for the first time, and actually casting ballots. *The Atlantic* reported in a November 6, 2016, article that early voting from young adults age eighteen to twenty-nine totaled 3.3 million, a surge of 188 percent compared to 2014. Also impressive was the advocacy by March for our Lives. According to Alison Durkee, March for our Lives partnered with HeadCount, to register more than 4,000 young voters in March 2018 (https://mic.com).

Although school is still out in terms of the longer-term impact of these and other advocacy groups, engaging voters around their passions in combination with early voting efforts can substantially improve turnout. While a vote by a young person fighting for gun control is not necessarily a vote for your school tax election, survey research clearly and consistently demonstrates that more young voters participating translates to more "yes" votes for school district ballot proposals.

KEY GET-OUT-THE-VOTE COMMITTEE RESPONSIBILITIES

The key activities of the get-out-the-vote committee are:

- Delivering every identified "yes" voter to the ballot box through either absentee voting or participation on election day;
- Completing reminder calls, email contacts, and targeted door-to door efforts on election day;
- Providing transportation to any "yes" voter needing a ride to the polls; and
- Providing childcare to any "yes" voter needing such assistance to vote.

Last, as detailed in chapter 4, plotting parent and voter history data on geovisual demographic maps also provides resources that can be used by the get-out-the-vote committee either on election day (if not prohibited by law) or in the days leading up to election day. Although most campaign committees use the telephone for get-out-the-vote efforts, demographic maps can help campaigners pinpoint specific areas, streets, or neighborhoods that warrant a targeted door-to-door effort to supplement reminder calls. Demographic mapping, for example, might identify ten adjacent homes on a particular street, all of which contain public school students with parents who are either unregistered or have very infrequent voting habits. The mapping provides the needed information to surgically deploy a team of volunteers to a specific grouping of homes to improve get-out-the-vote results. In our experience, we have seen school tax campaigns pull anywhere from 33 to 95 percent of its supporters to the polls depending on the effectiveness of the campaign and the get-out-the-vote committee's execution.

Dealing with Organized Opposition

Many factors will influence if and when organized opposition might emerge in your campaign. If it does, you need to be prepared to deal with the distraction it will produce. The word "distraction" is used with great purpose here because the first thing opposition produces is distraction. All of the energy your campaign committee has poured into its efforts to promote and communicate could be rechanneled overnight into phone calls, email exchanges, and emergency meetings intended to counter opposition. As a result, your opponents have the ability to waste many valuable volunteer hours.

To blunt this effect, some campaigns have organized a "rear guard" to deal with the distraction opponents can generate. The members of this part of the campaign team are responsible for handling anything done by the opposition while the rest of the campaign continues to execute the plan it developed to inform, identify, and reinforce "yes" votes. By absorbing the impact that the opposition is attempting to land on campaign leadership, the rear guard helps keep the overall campaign on track and on target.

The composition and nature of the opponents that emerge in your district will drive the message they will present to the community. Often, this will not be an effort to communicate so much as an attempt to disrupt your communication efforts and confuse the voters. Remember that your opponent's primary goal is to defeat your tax proposal, not engage in a debate. While you must deliver clear, concise information to the voters to generate "yes" votes, an opposition group only needs to create confusion and doubt to create "no" votes. As a result, you need to ensure the campaign maintains its focus and does not let opposition take it off plan or off message. It is essential that the bulk of the campaign's energy keeps moving toward victory on election day.

If organized opposition emerges during your campaign, there are some specific rules we suggest you follow. First, make sure your campaign sticks to its campaign and communications plan. You may need to modify that plan to deal with the elements the opposition has introduced. But, if you abandon your campaign plan entirely, you have, in essence, turned the leadership of your effort over to the opposition.

Second, respond to items the opposition introduces in a way that keeps your primary message in front of the voters. This can be accomplished by following the 80/20 rule: 80 percent of your response should present your primary argument for the tax proposal, and only 20 percent of your response should be used to address the opposition's arguments. In doing so, however, you should ensure you do not overrespond. For example, instead of assuming you need to use every medium available to you, the campaign should respond only in the medium selected by the opponents. You want to avoid situations where your campaign introduces the arguments of your opponents to voters who might otherwise never come across those ideas.

Third, do not be afraid to dismiss the opposition as individuals who are opposed to all tax proposals or to the basic idea that we should have good public schools in the United States. Never assume the voters of your district know that what at first appears to be new ideas introduced by the opposition might in fact be long-standing antitax or antigovernment arguments that can be found in abundance on the Internet. You also may need to tell your voters not to be confused by the misinformation introduced by organized opposition.

Fourth, remember your best weapon is the "light" created by clear, concise information about the district's needs and its tax proposal. Opposition groups do their best work in the shadows where their innuendos and assertions can fester unchallenged. Do not be afraid to draw the opposition into the bright "light" of the public forum. This does not mean you immediately challenge them to a debate. Rather, it does mean you take as much information about them, their background, and your proposal to the press and to community leaders.

You also make sure all your volunteers and district staff are well briefed and prepared to confidently rebut any of the opponent's statements should they hear them repeated among their friends and neighbors.

Finally, remember that all of your actions are part of a political campaign. Election day is the goal, and every action you take must be planned and executed to move your proposal one step closer to that goal. You may feel a strong impulse to educate and explain, but you must resist that impulse until election day. Instead, measure and plan your responses to blunt the impact of your opponents and achieve your original goal—stronger classroom programs or better school facilities for students.

If we were to summarize this chapter in just two words, it would be "Campaigning matters!" It is incumbent upon the superintendent and campaign leadership to understand and avail themselves of both research and best practice. Once the campaign plan is developed, it is vital that it be executed in world-class fashion—coordinated between the school district and citizens' campaign committee—based not only on research and successful practice but also on the unique culture of your school community. The margins between winning and losing are just too slim to do anything less.

Note

1. Portions of this chapter originally appeared in "School Finance elections: Hip-Hop to Victory," Don E. Lifto, PhD, published in *School Business Affairs*, Association of School Business Officials International, December 2004.

A Final Thought

The title for the third edition of this book adds the words "In the New Normal," challenging the authors to think about what's the same and what's different since publication of the previous two editions in 2004 and 2010. What has not changed in our experience is the fact that passing school tax referenda is one of the most challenging leadership responsibilities for superintendents and school districts. Doing so still requires thoughtful and meticulous planning grounded in research and best practices and tailored to the culture of your community.

The fabric of the new normal for school tax elections—while always in flux based on a variety of strategic, nonstrategic, and critical factors—is increasingly woven in strands of the following: demographics and aging of the baby boomers, diminished size of parent households, impact of online media, challenge of effectively communicating and engaging citizens in an increasingly hectic environment, and the increasing impact of state and national politics on what previously had been primarily local initiatives. Meeting the operating, technology, and facility needs of school districts and the students and families served in your community will depend upon the ability of school leaders to plan and execute tax referenda within this more demanding context.

It is our sincere hope that our research and experience working with school leaders and districts for more than thirty years will provide not only strategies and resources for planning but also the needed energy and determination to achieve success in meeting needs of students, families, and public schools in the future.

We express our sincere and heartfelt appreciation to the many professional colleagues over the years for their support, guidance, and willingness to share ideas. Thanks also to our clients who gave us the opportunity to serve.

Appendix A

School Referendum Research and Planning

Don E. Lifto, PhD

NATIONAL PRESENTATIONS

"School Tax Elections: Lifto's Top 10." Presenter at Tech Learning/SchoolBond-Finder Conference in Austin, Texas, 2019.

"School Tax Elections Planning Resources: Lifto's Top 10." Presenter at RTM Education Conference in Orlando, Florida, 2018.

"By the Numbers: Harnessing the Power of Voter Targeting for Successful School Tax Elections." Presenter at Association of School Business Officials International in Orlando, Florida, 2018.

"Why Referenda Fail: Research and Best Practices for Success." Presenter at Association of School Business Officials International in Denver, Colorado, 2017.

"Gaining Community Support for Tax Referenda in the 'New Normal.'" Presenter at the National Association of Municipal Advisors in Charlotte, North Carolina, 2016.

"Passing Tax Referenda in the 'New Normal.'" Presenter at the National Center for Education Research and Technology in Jacksonville, Florida, 2016.

"Using Technology to Target Voters in School Tax Elections." Presenter at the Association of School Business Officials International in Orlando, Florida, 2014.

"School Referenda and Organized Opposition: Research and Best Practices to Plan and Manage for Success at the Ballot Box." Presenter at the National School Boards Association in Boston, Massachusetts, 2012.

"Politics, Perspectives and School Tax Elections." Presenter at the Association of School Business Officials International in Seattle, Washington, 2011.

"Success in School Tax Elections: Micro-Targeting." Presenter at the National School Boards Association in San Francisco, California, 2011.

"Using Technology Applications to Micro-Target Messages in a Referendum Campaign." Presenter at the Association of School Business Officials International in Orlando, Florida, 2010.

"School Tax Elections: Twitter Your Way to Victory." Presenter at the American Association of School Administrators' National Conference in Phoenix, Arizona, 2010.

"School Tax Elections and the Internet: New Strategies for Technology-Savvy Voters." Presenter at National School Boards Association in Chicago, Illinois, 2010.

"School Finance Elections: Preparing for Organized Opposition." Presenter at the American Association of School Administrators' Summer Leadership Conference in St. Louis, Missouri, 2008.

"Precinct 5: How Data Turned an Election Defeat to Victory." Presenter at National School Boards Association in San Diego, California, 2005.

"Precinct 5: How Data Turned an Election Defeat to Victory." Presenter at Association of School Business Officials International in Cincinnati, Ohio, 2004.

"Data Driven Decision Making for School Finance Elections? Yes!" Presenter at the National School Boards Association National Convention in Orlando, Florida, 2004.

"School Finance Elections." Presenter at the Association of School Business Officials International National Convention in Charlotte, North Carolina, 2003.

"Comprehensive Planning Model for School Bond and Operating Levies." Presenter at the National School Boards Association National Convention in San Francisco, California, 2003.

November 6, 2001 . . . Budget Battles at the Ballot Box." Presenter at the Association of School Business Officials International National Convention in Phoenix, Arizona, 2002.

"Drivers of Successful Bond and Operating Levies . . . Q4C at the Foundation." Presenter at the Association of School Business Officials International National Convention in Baltimore, Maryland, 2001.

"So You Lost the Election . . . Now What?" Presenter at the American Association of School Administrators' National Convention in San Francisco, California, 2000.

"Strategic Planning and Opinion Sampling: Constructive Interplay for Successful Referenda." Presenter at the American Association of School Administrators' National Convention in Orlando, Florida, 1993.

Appendix B
School Referendum Research and Planning
Don E. Lifto, PhD

BOOKS AND PUBLICATIONS IN NATIONAL JOURNALS

Books

School Tax Elections: Planning for Success in the New Normal, Third Edition, Don E. Lifto, PhD, & Barbara Nicol, APR, published by Rowman & Littlefield & the American Association of School Administrators, 2019.

School Finance Elections: A Comprehensive Planning Model for Success, Second Edition, Don E. Lifto, PhD, & J. Bradford Senden, PhD, published by Rowman & Littlefield & the American Association of School Administrators, 2010.

School Finance Elections: A Comprehensive Planning Model for Success, Don E. Lifto, PhD, & J. Bradford Senden, PhD, published by Scarecrow Press & the American Association of School Administrators, 2004.

Articles Published in National Journals

"By the Numbers: A School District's Tax Elections," Don E. Lifto, PhD, published in *The School Administrator*, American Association of School Administrators, December 2017.

"Voter Targeting and School Tax Elections: Data and Technology Strategies to Mine Support and Deliver 'Yes' Votes," Don E. Lifto, PhD, & J. Bradford Senden, PhD, *School Business Affairs*, Association of School Business Officials International, September 2015.

"Insights and Implications: Mining Data from Scientific, Random-Sample Surveys," Don E. Lifto, PhD, & Chris Deets, *American School Board Journal*, National School Board Association, January 2015.

"Party Politics and School Tax Elections," Don E. Lifto, PhD, & J. Bradford Senden, PhD, published in *The School Administrator*, American Association of School Administrators, March 2012.

"School Tax Elections: Testing Messages and Targeting Voters," J. Bradford Senden, PhD, & Don E. Lifto, PhD, published in *School Business Affairs*, Association of School Business Officials International, December 2010.

"Eight Tips for Planning and Executing Successful School Tax Elections," Don E. Lifto, PhD, & J. Bradford Senden, PhD, published in *The Leader's Edge*, American Association of School Administrators, October 2009.

"Transforming White Light into Rainbows: Segmentation Strategies for Successful School Tax Elections," J. Bradford Senden, PhD, & Don E. Lifto, PhD, published in *School Business Affairs*, Association of School Business Officials International, May 2009.

"The Forgotten Alumni," Don E. Lifto, PhD, & J. Bradford Senden, PhD, published in *American School Board Journal*, National School Board Association, October 2008.

"Managing Organized Opposition," Don E. Lifto, PhD, & J. Bradford Senden, PhD, published in *The School Administrator*, American Association of School Administrators, April 2008.

"Watch Your Language: Words to Win By in your Next School Finance Campaign," Don E. Lifto, PhD, & J. Bradford Senden, PhD, published in *The School Administrator*, American Association of School Administrators, February 2006.

"The Case of Precinct 5," Don E. Lifto, PhD, & J. Bradford Senden, PhD, published in *American School Board Journal*, National School Board Association, April 2005.

"School Finance Elections: Hip-Hop to Victory," Don E. Lifto, PhD, published in *School Business Affairs*, Association of School Business Officials International, December 2004.

"Examining Elections Past," Don E. Lifto, PhD, & J. Bradford Senden, PhD, published in *The School Administrator*, American Association of School Administrators, January 2004.

"Concentric Canvassing . . . Finding Success from the Inside Out," Don E. Lifto, PhD, & J. Bradford Senden, PhD, published in *School Business Affairs*, Association of School Business Officials International, November 2002.

"Lessons from the Bond Battlefield," Don E. Lifto, PhD, published in *American School Board Journal*, National School Board Association, November 2001.

"Drivers of Successful Bond and Operating Levies . . . Q4C at the Foundation, Don E. Lifto, PhD, & William Morris, PhD, originally published in *School Business Affairs*, Association of School Business Officials International, October 2000.

"A Matter of Wealth: The Slippery Slope of Testing and Accountability," Don E. Lifto, PhD, published in *The School Administrator*, American Association of School Administrators, January 2000.

"What Do Parents Want?" Don E. Lifto, PhD, published in *American School Board Journal*, National School Board Association, January 2000.

"So You've Lost the Bond or Referendum Election—What Do You Do Now?" Don E. Lifto, PhD, & Rolf W. Parsons, PhD, published in *School Business Affairs*, Association of School Business Officials International, November 1998.

Bibliography

Allen, A. L. (1985). Predictors of voting behavior in school financial referenda (Doctoral dissertation). *Dissertation Abstracts International, 47,* 719.

Beckham, J. D. (2001). An examination of the influence of technology inclusion in determining the outcome of school bond issue elections in Oklahoma (Doctoral dissertation). *Dissertation Abstracts International, 62,* 85.

Blount, K. D. (1991). The relationship between school tax election outcomes, selected population characteristics, and selected campaign strategies in Louisiana from 1985–1990 (Doctoral dissertation). *Dissertation Abstracts International, 52,* 3180.

Bolman, L. G., & Deal, T. E. (1991). *Reframing organization: Artistry, choice, and leadership.* San Francisco, CA: Jossey-Bass.

Brummer, K. C. (1999). School bond elections in Iowa: An analysis of factors, strategies, and policies that influence outcomes (Doctoral dissertation). *Dissertation Abstracts International, 61,* 2538.

Chandler, J. A. (1989). A comparison of the predictability rates of the Lutz dissatisfaction and school bond election models of local school district politics in selected Oklahoma school districts, 1971–1989 (Doctoral dissertation). *Dissertation Abstracts International, 52,* 30.

Clemens, A. D. (2003). Issues and related strategies used in successful school facilities bond elections in seven selected Orange County school districts between June 2000 to March 2002 (Doctoral dissertation). Retrieved from ProQuest Dissertations and Theses (Section 0476, Part 0514).

Corrick, C. C. (1995). Voter perceptions, information, and demographic characteristics as critical factors in successful and unsuccessful bond referenda in selected Kansas school districts: 1988–1990 (Doctoral dissertation). *Dissertation Abstracts International, 56,* 2054.

Dalton, R. A. (1995). Local general obligation bonds: Factors which have influenced the outcome of school district elections (Doctoral dissertation). *Dissertation Abstracts International, 57,* 44.

Day, D. V. (1996). Influences on a community college bond election: A case study (Doctoral dissertation). *Dissertation Abstracts International, 57,* 2336.

Dunbar, D. W. (1991). A comparison of mail ballot elections and polling place elections for school bond issues in Kansas (elections) (Doctoral dissertation). *Dissertation Abstracts International, 52,* 3180.

Etheredge, F. D. (1989). *School boards and the ballot box.* Alexandria, VA: National School Boards Association.

Faltys, D. J. (2006). Factors influencing the successful passage of a school bond referendum as identified by selected voters in the Navasota Independent School District in Texas (Doctoral dissertation). Retrieved from ProQuest Dissertations and Theses (Section 0803, Part 0277).

Flanigan, W. H., & Zingale, N. H. (1998). *Political behavior and the American electorate* (9th ed.). Washington, DC: CQ Press.

Franklin, G. A. (1997). School finance campaigns: Strategies and other factors related to success (voters) (Doctoral dissertation). *Dissertation Abstracts International, 58,* 1595.

Friedland, H. A. (2002). The ecology of school bond elections: Factors associated with election results in New Jersey (Doctoral dissertation). Retrieved from ProQuest Dissertations and Theses (Section 0055, Part 0514).

Galton, L. L. (1996). Understanding the reasons for and impact of one small Massachusetts community's lack of fiscal support for its local school system, 1990–1993 (Doctoral dissertation). *Dissertation Abstracts International, 57,* 944.

Geurink, G. (2008). An analysis of factors leading to the passage of school district finance referenda within the State of Wisconsin (Doctoral dissertation). Retrieved from ProQuest Dissertations and Theses (Section 0501, Part 0277).

Grady-Hahn, L. F. (1999) School levy failures: A look at causes and cures (Master's dissertation). Retrieved from ProQuest Dissertations and Theses (Section 6200, Part 0514).

Hallene, A. F., Jr. (1999). Development of a logistic regression methodology for predicting K-12 education tax rate increase referenda outcomes by individual school district (Doctoral dissertation). Retrieved from ProQuest Dissertations and Theses (Section 0096, Part 0546).

Henderson, J. F., Jr. (1986). Revenue election campaign strategies used in Colorado school districts which conducted successful and unsuccessful elections for 1981–1985 (Doctoral dissertation). *Dissertation Abstracts International, 58,* 2542.

Hickey, W. D. (2004). A survey of superintendent emotional intelligence as a factor in bond election outcomes (Doctoral dissertation). Retrieved from ProQuest Dissertations and Theses (Section 6340, Part 0514).

Hinson, J. L. (2001). A study of the relationship between the outcome of school district bond issue elections and selected variables (Doctoral dissertation). *Dissertation Abstracts International, 62,* 1652.

Hockersmith, D. C. (2001). Strategies used by school district superintendents, chief business officials, and school board members to achieve acquisition of a general obligation bond (Doctoral dissertation). *Dissertation Abstracts International, 61,* 4627.

Kimbrough, R. B., & Nunnery, M. Y. (1971). *Politics, power, polls, and school elections.* Berkeley, CA: McCutchan.

Kinsall, M. L. (2000). A study of the effects of election campaign strategies on successful passage of tax levies (Doctoral dissertation). Retrieved from ProQuest Dissertations and Theses (Section 0193, Part 0277).

Lake, C. C., & Callbeck Harper, P. (1987). *Public opinion polling: A handbook for public interest and citizen advocacy groups.* Washington, DC: Island.

Lifto, D. E. (2001, November). Lessons from the bond battlefield. *American School Board Journal.*

———. (2005, March–April). School finance elections: Hip-hop to victory. *School Business Affairs.*

Lifto, D. E., & Morris, W. (2000). Drivers of successful bond and operating levies . . . Q4C at the foundation. *School Business Affairs, 66*(10), 15–17.

———. (2001, March–April). Q4C referendums. *Minnesota School Boards Association Journal.*

Lifto, D. E., & Parsons, R. W. (1998, November). So you've lost the bond or referendum election—what do you do now? *School Business Affairs.*

Lifto, D. E., & Senden, J. B. (2002, February–March). Budget battles at the ballot box. *Minnesota School Boards Association Journal.*

———. (2002, November). Concentric canvassing: Finding success from the inside out. *School Business Affairs.*

———. (2003, February). Finding success at the ballot box. *Managing School Business.*

———. (2004, January). Examining elections past. *School Administrator.*

———. (2004). *School finance elections: A comprehensive planning model for success.* Scarecrow Press and the American Association of School Administrators.

———. (2005, April). The case of precinct 5. *American School Board Journal.*

———. (2006, February). Watch your language: Words to win by in your next school finance campaign. *School Administrator.*

———. (2008, April). Managing organized opposition. *School Administrator.*

———. (2009, March–April). Understanding alumni parents and school voting tendencies. *Minnesota School Boards Association Journal.*

———. (2009, May). Transforming white light into rainbows: Segmentation strategies for successful school tax elections. *School Business Affairs.*

Lode, M. D. (1999). Factors affecting the outcomes of school bond elections in Iowa (Doctoral dissertation). *Dissertation Abstracts International, 60,* 2310.

Mobley, L. B. (2007). An anatomy of an unsuccessful school bond election in a rural school district (Doctoral dissertation). Mississippi State University.

National School Public Relations Association. (2002). *Raising the bar for school PR: New standards for the school public relations profession.* Rockville, MD: Author.

Neill, S. W. (2003). The identification of effective strategies for bond campaigns in Kansas school districts: An analysis of the beliefs of superintendents who conducted bond issue campaigns (Doctoral dissertation). Retrieved from Pro-Quest Dissertations and Theses (Section 0260, Part 0514).

Pappalardo, J. W., Jr. (2005). Strategies used by superintendents, chief business officials, and school board members in successful Proposition 39 general education bond elections (Doctoral dissertation). Retrieved from ProQuest Dissertations and Theses (Section 0476, Part 0277).

Phillips, C. T. (1995). An investigation of strategies related to successful and un-successful campaigns for passage of school operating issues in Ohio (Doctoral dissertation). *Dissertation Abstracts International, 56,* 1610.

Piele, P., & Hall, J. (1973). *Budgets, bonds, and ballots.* Lexington, MA: Heath.

Pullium, T. N. (1983). A study of selected factors associated with the success and failure of school bond referenda in the state of Georgia during the decade of the 1970s (Doctoral dissertation). *Dissertation Abstracts International, 44,* 1281.

Schrom, J. W. (2004). School-community interaction and communication dur-ing a general obligation bond election (Doctoral dissertation). University of California, Riverside.

Sclafani, S. (1985). The determinants of school budget election outcomes in New York State: A forecasting model (Doctoral dissertation). *Dissertation Abstracts International, 47,* 83.

Stockton, D. J. (1996). Influences contributing to the successful passage of a school bond referendum in the Conroe Independent School District (Texas, tax levy) (Doctoral dissertation). *Dissertation Abstracts International, 57,* 2312.

True, N. B. (1996). Factors affecting the passage or defeat of California school districts' parcel tax measures between 1983 and 1994 (Doctoral dissertation). *Dissertation Abstracts International, 57,* 1496.

Wellstone Action. (2005). *Politics the Wellstone way.* Minneapolis, MN: Univer-sity of Minnesota Press.

Werner, M. J. (2012). An analysis of the New Jersey Public School District school bond referendum process: A historical case study of the Egg Harbor Township School District Bond Referendum of 2004–05. (Doctoral disserta-tion). University of Pennsylvania.

Williamson, S. G. (1997). Factors influencing voter behavior in school board elec-tions (Doctoral dissertation). *Dissertation Abstracts International, 58,* 3015.

ADDITIONS TO BIBLIOGRAPHY

Internet Sites

American Association of Public Opinion Research https://www.aapor.org/.
Grassroots Solutions http://www.grassrootssolutions.com/.
GuideK12 Geovisual Analytics for Education https://guidek12.com/.
National School Public Relations Association https://www.nspra.org.
SchoolBondFinder https://www.schoolbondfinder.com/.

Books

Green, D. P., & Gerber, A. S. (2004). *Get out the vote! How to increase voter turnout.* Washington, DC: Brookings Institution.
Green, D. P., & Gerber, A. S. (2015). *Get out the vote! How to increase voter turnout.* Washington, DC: Brookings Institution.

Lifto's Journal Articles

Lifto, D. E. (2017, December). By the numbers: A school district's tax elections. *The School Administrator.*

Lifto and Senden's Journal Articles

Lifto, D. E., & Senden, J. B. (2010, December). School tax elections: Testing messages and targeting voters. *School Business Affairs.*
Lifto, D. E., & Senden, J. B. (2011, May–June). Planning and executing successful referenda in the new normal: Overcoming economic, political, and demographic challenges. *Minnesota School Boards Association Journal.*
Lifto, D. E., & Senden, J. B. (2012, March). Party politics and school tax elections. *The School Administrator.*
Lifto, D. E., & Senden, J. B. (2015, September). Voter targeting and school tax elections: Data and technology strategies to mine support and deliver "yes" votes. *School Business Affairs.*

Lifto and Deets's Journal Articles

Lifto, D. E., & Deets, C. (2015, January). Insights and implications: Mining data from scientific, random-sample surveys. *American School Board Journal.*

Other Journal Article

Anthony, A., & Skaggs, D. E. (2002, August). Winning with young voters: How to reach—and motivate—30 million missing voters under 30. *Campaigns & Elections*, 22–29.

Citations for Dissertations

Benzaquen, E. Y. (2016). School bond referenda reloaded: An examination of a school district in passing a subsequent bond referendum after failing to pass previous bond referenda (Doctoral dissertation). Retrieved from ProQuest Dissertations and Theses (10124139).

Godown, M. P. (2011). Factors influencing the successful passage of a school bond referendum as identified by New Jersey school superintendents (Doctoral dissertation). Retrieved from ProQuest Dissertations and Theses (3452451).

Heitzman, S. M. (2018). Variables influencing the successful passage of school bond referenda as identified by selected stakeholders in Texas (Doctoral dissertation). Retrieved from http://hdl.handle.net/2152/65657 .

Hoh, T. H. (2017). Factors associated with passing school district capital project referenda in Wisconsin, 2011–2016 (Doctoral dissertation). Retrieved from ProQuest Dissertations and Theses (10686746).

Kobren, M. E. (2015). Taxing ourselves: Understanding school tax elections (Doctoral dissertation). Retrieved from ProQuest Dissertations and Theses (3725801).

Kraus, B. W. (2009). A descriptive analysis of selected community stakeholder opinions regarding potentially critical factors in school bond referenda success or failure in Kansas during the years 2004–2007 (Doctoral dissertation). Retrieved from ProQuest Dissertations and Theses (3389839).

Kreimer, K. (2017). The identification of effective strategies used in successfully passing tax elections in Missouri and Arkansas school districts (Doctoral dissertation). Retrieved from ProQuest Dissertations and Theses (10268532).

Lambert, W. A. (2012). Superintendent perceptions of the success and failure of school construction referendums from 2008–2010 in the state of Indiana (Doctoral dissertation). Retrieved from ProQuest Dissertations and Theses (3507502).

Meszaros, I. S. (2010). The political economy of California school district parcel tax elections (Doctoral dissertation). Retrieved from ProQuest Dissertations and Theses (3403741).

Moore, J. C. (2018). A phenomenological narrative study of selected Texas superintendent perceptions as to why recent school bond elections were successful in their school district (Doctoral dissertation). Retrieved from ProQuest Dissertations and Theses (10808583).

Morris, E. (2016). Superintendent perceptions of critical facets related to successful and unsuccessful school bond elections in Texas public school districts (Doctoral dissertation). Retrieved from ProQuest Dissertation and Theses (10291005).

Packer, C. D. (2013). School referenda and Ohio Department of Education typologies: An investigation of the outcomes of first attempt school operating levies from 2002–2010 (Doctoral dissertation). Retrieved from ProQuest Dissertations and Theses (3599104).

Russo, C. J. (2010). Planning a school construction referendum: A case study of a small rural school district in southern New Jersey (Doctoral dissertation). Retrieved from ProQuest Dissertations and Theses (3401565).

Sargent, A. C. (2014). Factors that affect the outcome of a general fund referendum in Indiana (Doctoral dissertation). Retrieved from ProQuest Dissertations and Theses (3702090).

Stauffacher, A. N. (2012). Strategies and factors influencing public school district referendums (Doctoral dissertation). Retrieved from ProQuest Dissertations and Theses (3524027).

Sullivan, K. E. (1993). A case study of an effective 1988 school finance referendum campaign by an Illinois public school district: Tremont, Illinois (Doctoral dissertation). Retrieved from ProQuest Dissertations and Theses (3452451).

Werner, M. J. (2012). An analysis of New Jersey Public School District school bond referenda process: An historical case study of the Egg Harbor Township School District bond referendum of 2004/05 (Doctoral dissertation). Retrieved from ProQuest Dissertation and Theses (3510985).

Wheatley, V. A. (2012). The relationship between components of the Ohio local school district report card and the outcome of a school tax levy (Doctoral dissertation). Retrieved from ProQuest Dissertations and Theses (3534593).

About the Authors

Don E. Lifto is a consultant with Springsted Inc., a public finance and consulting firm based in St. Paul. Previously, he was a school superintendent in Minnesota for twenty-five years, having served in rural, suburban, and intermediate districts. Lifto is a frequent presenter on school tax election strategies at AASA, NSBA, and ASBO and has more than a dozen articles published on related topics in national journals.

Barb Nicol, APR, has more than thirty years of experience in the communications field. She founded Barbara Nicol Public Relations in 1990 and focuses her work on providing strategic and high-quality communications expertise to school districts and education-related organizations. Previously, Barb was the communications director for the Minnesota Private College Council and held several positions at Sheggeby Advertising, a business-to-business advertising agency.